LANDSCAPE TREES AND SHRUBS

Selection, Use and Management

038793

LANDSMANS BOOKSHOP LTD.
Tel/Fax +44 (0)1885-483420
www.landsmans.co.uk

For Helen Forrest

LANDSCAPE TREES AND SHRUBS
Selection, Use and Management

Mary Forrest

UCD School of Biology and Environmental Science
Agriculture and Food Science Centre
University College Dublin
Belfield
Dublin 4
Ireland

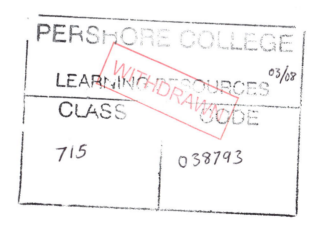

PERSHORE COLLEGE

LEARNING RESOURCES   03/08

WITHDRAWN

CLASS   CODE

715   038793

www.cabi.org

Pershore College

CABI is a trading name of CAB International

CABI Head Office
Nosworthy Way
Wallingford
Oxon OX10 8DE
UK

Tel: +44 (0)1491 832111
Fax: +44 (0)1491 833508
E-mail: cabi@cabi.org
Website: www.cabi.org

CABI North American Office
875 Massachusetts Avenue
7th Floor
Cambridge, MA 02139
USA

Tel: +1 617 395 4056
Fax: +1 617 354 6875
E-mail: cabi-nao@cabi.org

© M. Forrest 2006. All rights reserved. No part of this publication may be reproduced in any form or by any means, electronically, mechanically, by photocopying, recording or otherwise, without the prior permission of the copyright owners.

A catalogue record for this book is available from the British Library, London, UK.

A catalogue record for this book is available from the Library of Congress, Washington DC, USA.

ISBN-10: 1 84593 054 1
ISBN-13: 978 1 84593 054 7

Typeset by Columns Design Ltd, Reading
Printed and bound by Athenaeum Press, Gateshead

Contents

Preface and Acknowledgements

Becoming familiar with all kinds of garden plants was a challenge for me when a student gardener. Obtain a good nursery catalogue and learn two plants a day was the advice given. It was valuable advice, and plant knowledge improved over time, but it was a haphazard method of learning plants. One day, the then taxonomist at the National Botanic Gardens, Dublin, brought students to the Family Beds, an area in the Gardens, and explained how plants were classified into families. One student, at least, was captivated by this system of classification and saw it as a method of recognizing and learning about plants. Some years later, while on visits to rhododendron gardens, members of the Royal Horticultural Society's Rhododendron, Camellia and Magnolia Group would explain to fellow members how rhododendrons were classified. While this classification served a botanical purpose, it was apparent that groups of species of rhododendrons (known as subsections) had certain common horticultural attributes, such as size of shrub, time of flowering and suitability for certain situations. As a university lecturer with a brief to develop courses in Plant Materials for undergraduates, it became evident to me that most of the trees and shrubs cultivated in urban and rural situations belong to a limited range of families. It also became clear that general statements about the use and management of these families could be made. In the course I subsequently developed, the schema of presenting plants by families dovetails with an examination of plants by the function they serve, such as hedges, ground cover and parkland trees.

For horticultural undergraduates in University College Dublin, CAB Abstracts (now CAB Direct – online) were a source of information for projects and reports. Many years later, an editor from CAB International called at my office, and we spoke about books. 'Had I an idea for a book?' asked Tim Hardwick. 'Yes,' and here it is.

This book would not have been written without the information garnered over many years from my own lecturers and fellow plant people and shaped by my students.

Acknowledgements

I am grateful to the following: Professor Jeremy Gray, UCD School of Biology and Environmental Science, University College Dublin, Ms Anne James, Talbot Botanic Gardens, Malahide Castle, and Peter MacDonald, Scottish Agricultural College (SAC), Auchincruive, Ayr, Scotland, who read drafts of this work.

Tom Moore of the UCD School of Biology and Environmental Science scanned images of my 35 mm slides. The original drawings by Kathy Saunders in Chapter 2 capture the innate characteristics and qualities of trees. The original drawings by Rosemary Wise of leaves, fruit and flowers of a selection of trees in Chapter 4 have been used with permission from CABI, the artist and Peter Savill.

Finally my thanks to Tim Hardwick and his colleagues at CABI, who turned a manuscript into a book.

Mary Forrest
University College Dublin
November 2005

Introduction

The selection, use and management of trees and shrubs is common to the careers of landscape architects, landscape managers, horticulturists, nursery stock producers and garden centre managers.

In Britain, native flowering plants and ferns number some 1500 species, while in Ireland about 1000 species are native (Scannell and Synnott, 1987). However the range of introduced or exotic plants is much greater. Over the centuries, plants introduced from the temperate regions of the world have become part of the garden flora and some have become naturalized in the wild. The numbers of different plants in the living collections of the following organizations are: Royal Botanic Gardens, Kew, 31,619; Royal Horticultural Society, 24,965; Royal Botanic Garden Edinburgh, 20,390; and National Botanic Gardens Glasnevin, Dublin, 20,000 (Walter, 2001). Some 73,000 plants available in nurseries in Britain and Ireland are listed in the *RHS Plant Finder 2005-2006* (Lord, 2005). While the living collections include plants in indoor and outdoor cultivation and the *RHS Plant Finder* lists all kinds of garden plants, including fruit and ferns, there is a large discrepancy between these numbers and the number of different trees and shrubs commonly grown in landscape schemes.

Thoday (1996) defined a landscape plant as 'capable of establishing and growing to produce the design intent under the relatively adverse conditions and low maintenance inputs generally encountered on development sites'. It is characterized by the following qualities: long aesthetic lifespan; year-round appearance; predictable growth rate; suitable and predictable gross morphology; a degree of tolerance to initial site conditions; tolerance of long-term site conditions; low maintenance demands; safety; resistance to some pests and diseases; and low fecundity.

Hitchmough (1996) estimated that no more than 1000 taxa were cultivated in public and commercial landscapes, with 30 taxa in regular use. Thoday's (1996) estimate was lower: 200 were used in any quantity, with

© M. Forrest 2006. *Landscape Trees and Shrubs: Selection, Use and Management* (M. Forrest)

some nurseries reporting that six trees and 15 shrubs comprised 75% of orders for landscape plants. Nor is this situation limited to Britain; in a survey of trees used in European cities, three to five genera accounted for 50–70% of all street trees planted (Pauliet *et al.*, 2002). Reasons given by Hitchmough (1996) for the narrow range of plants grown in landscape schemes are lack of commercial availability and users' lack of knowledge of the diversity and characteristics of the cultivated flora.

Books such as *Common Families of Flowering Plants* (Hickey and King, 1997) and *The Identification of Flowering Plant Families* (Cullen, 1997) describe diagnostic features and classification and briefly mention ornamental uses of the families described. Many horticultural books, for example, *The Hillier Manual of Trees and Shrubs* (Anon., 2003) and *Trees and Shrubs Hardy in the British Isles* (Bean, 1976–1980), list trees and shrubs in alphabetical order by genus. *The Planting Design Handbook* (Robinson, 2004) discusses the process of planting design in great detail; while emphasizing the necessity of plant knowledge, it is not discussed in any detail.

If one takes the standard range of plants used in urban and rural situations in Western Europe, most belong to a limited number of plant families and within these plant families some genera contribute significantly to landscape schemes. Reviewing these plant families, it is possible to make general comments about their suitability in landscape design schemes and their management in such schemes.

What is presented in this book is a horticultural overlay of the main plant families from temperate regions cultivated in landscape schemes. The purpose is to provide a schema by which readers can become familiar with the range of plants available in the landscape industry and their uses in landscape schemes. When designing or managing planting schemes, they should be familiar with the diagnostic, cultivation and management characteristics of a range of genera. They would be able to prepare planting designs suitable for a prevailing site. They could assess new species seen in nursery catalogues, in planting schemes or in plant collections. This approach would be useful for professionals specializing in nursery stock to appraise new material for the garden centre business, or for arboriculturists who undertake tree surveys and horticulturists preparing inventories of cultivated plants.

Chapter 1 gives a description of the functional uses of vegetation. Chapter 2 lists the ornamental attributes of trees and shrubs. An introduction to plant nomenclature is given in Chapter 3. In Chapter 4, 38 plant families are described according to their identification, functional use and management in landscape schemes. Examples of particular schemes or plant associations seen by the author are included and the reader is encouraged to seek out and review examples of plants and planting schemes in their locality. Chapter 5 provides a synthesis of the previous chapter and describes how planting schemes are developed with particular reference to trees and shrubs.

References

Anon. (2003) *The Hillier Manual of Trees and Shrubs.* David and Charles, Newton Abbot, UK.

Bean, W.J. (1976–1980) *Trees and Shrubs Hardy in the British Isles*, 8th edn. John Murray, London.

Cullen, J. (1997) *The Identification of Flowering Plant Families.* Cambridge University Press, Cambridge.

Hickey, M. and King, C. (1997) *Common Families of Flowering Plants.* Cambridge University Press, Cambridge.

Hitchmough, J. (1996) Where are the new plants to come from? Harnessing nature and science. In: Thoday, P. and Wilson, J. (eds) *Landscape Plants.* Cheltenham and Gloucester College of Higher Education, Cheltenham, UK, pp. 21–30.

Lord, T. (ed.) (2005) *RHS Plant Finder 2005–2006*, Dorling Kindersley, London.

Pauliet, S., Jones, N., Garcia-Martin, G., Garcia-Valdecantos, J.L., Rivière, L.M., Vidal-Beaudet, L., Bodson, M. and Randrup, T. (2002) Tree establishment practice in towns and cities – results from a European survey. *Urban Forestry and Urban Greening* 1, 83–96.

Robinson, N. (2004) *Planting Design Handbook*, 2nd edn. Ashgate, Aldershot, UK.

Scannell, M. and Synnott, D. (1987) *Census Catalogue of the Flora of Ireland*, 2nd edn. Stationery Office, Dublin.

Thoday, P. (1996) Landscape plants. In: Thoday, P. and Wilson, J. (eds) *Landscape Plants.* Cheltenham and Gloucester College of Higher Education, Cheltenham, UK, pp. 1–9.

Walter, K. (2001) Overview of the living collection at RBGE. In: Govier, R., Walter, K., Chamberlain, D., Gardner, M., Thomas, P., Alexander, C., Maxwell, H. and Watson, M. (eds) *Catalogue of Plants 2001.* Royal Botanic Garden Edinburgh, Edinburgh, pp. ix–xxiii.

1 Functional Uses of Vegetation in Urban and Rural Areas

Perhaps one of the best ways to appreciate the use of vegetation in the landscape is to look at it from an aeroplane. Descending from the clouds, fields with boundaries of trees, forests and woods in regular or irregular patterns, housing estates speckled with trees, and public parks with woodland and copses of tall trees all come into view.

Trees and shrubs fulfil many functions in a natural or designed landscape, fulfilling one or several functions simultaneously. A row of tall trees in a city park can provide shade from sun or rain for members of the public, a nesting site for birds and filter noise and intercept particles of dust. A 25-m tall solitary *Quercus* (oak) tree in a field will shelter sheep or cattle and support a wide variety of insects.

In this chapter, four categories of functional use are discussed – design, environmental, engineering and aesthetic. The functional uses refer to plant assemblages, groups of trees, groups of trees and shrubs and what are referred to as planting schemes. These can include a hedge or hedgerow in a rural or semi-rural area, a shrubbery in a park, perimeter parkland planting in an estate, barrier planting in an industrial site, semi-natural schemes along roads and motorways, individual specimen trees or an avenue. While numerous examples are cited, readers are encouraged to seek out examples for themselves in their own locality. In the next chapter, the qualities or characteristics of an individual tree or shrub are discussed.

Design

When designing or managing a planting scheme of some size, a landscape designer or landscape manager must be aware of the roles or functions performed by the vegetation, i.e. trees, shrubs and other plants. Vegetation has

© M. Forrest 2006. *Landscape Trees and Shrubs: Selection, Use and Management*
(M. Forrest)

many functions in a natural or designed landscape and, indeed, a particular planting scheme can serve several functions at once.

Unity

In a housing estate, diverse architecture can be unified by a single type of tree, or a variety of trees can be used to give variation where the architectures of the houses or industrial buildings are identical.

Linkage

Trees can be seen as visual connectors, linking planting of trees in urban areas with those in suburban and periurban areas and with those in the surrounding countryside (Fig. 1.1).

Enframement

Examples include tall columnar trees used to mark an entrance to a site and in some suburban gardens a horizontal *Prunus serrulata* (Japanese cherry)

Fig. 1.1. In Plovdiv, Bulgaria, *Populus* trees link one green area with another and contrast with the angular outline of buildings. In the foreground the columnar trees serve as a foil for the tall columns.

used as a canopy over an entrance. In Windsor Great Park (England) an avenue of *Aesculus* (horse chestnut) and *Platanus* (plane) frames the view in one direction towards a statue of the Duke of Cumberland and in the other to Windsor Castle.

Emphasis

Vegetation can act as a backdrop, background or foil for other vegetation. At the Royal Botanic Garden, Edinburgh, a tall *Fagus* (beech) hedge serves as a backdrop to a multicoloured herbaceous border. At Kenwood, a historic park in north London, green woodland is a foil to a grey reclining figure by the sculptor Henry Moore. On a massive scale, trees formed the background to many of the 18th century landscape parks, such as Castle Howard in Yorkshire.

Directional

Over the centuries trees have been used to create a boulevard or promenade or grand entrance into a city or estate, the Champs-Elysées in Paris and the South Avenue at Stowe, the landscape park in Buckinghamshire, being two notable examples. Vegetation can indicate a change in the road or motorway to the motorist. For example, on part of the M50 around the city of Dublin, exits from the motorway are signalled by large block-planting of distinctive red- and yellow-stemmed *Cornus alba* and *Cornus sericea* 'Flaviramea' (dogwood).

Camouflage

Vegetation can be used to hide unsightly objects, such as delivery bays in shopping centres, car parks or oil tanks. It can also be used to soften harsh lines of buildings.

Making spaces

Vegetation is used to create, organize, define and delimit space. While walls can be used to make spaces or enclosures or serve as dividers and barriers, trees and shrubs can fulfil the same function (Fig. 1.2). Such enclosures can vary from low hedges, which create informal barriers, knee-high barriers, which deter people from walking but do not impede the view, to high hedges, which prevent a view of the surrounding areas. In industrial areas, tall barriers delineate one property from another, while in suburban areas, hedges often separate one garden from another. In rural areas hedgerows create multilayered field boundaries.

Fig. 1.2. Standard trees (*Ulmus*), feathered trees in hedgerows, hedges and mounds of soil define a car park in an urban forest (Almera, the Netherlands).

Environmental

Scientific techniques can quantify the functions of trees in the environment, especially in relation to the atmosphere.

Air quality

Trees replace carbon dioxide with oxygen and increase the moisture content in the atmosphere. They remove gaseous and particulate pollution from the surrounding atmosphere. A plantation 30-m deep gives almost complete dust interception and also reduces gaseous pollution (Innes, 1990). Trees can be described as carbon sinks. As they grow trees sequester carbon from carbon dioxide, thus reducing levels of atmospheric carbon dioxide. The offset potential of 200 ha of newly planted woodland in Edinburgh has been estimated to be 18,000–30,000 t of carbon (Anon., 1999). Bradshaw *et al.* (1995) state that a mature *Quercus* (oak) weighs at least 1.5 t and contains about 0.5 t of carbon. A study of the 21% tree cover of Oakland, California, estimated a tree carbon storage level of 11.0 t/ha (Nowak, 1993).

Originally designed to allow the plant to respire and photosynthesize, plant leaves have evolved to function as efficient gas exchange systems, having a large surface area bearing pores and with an internal structure that allows rapid diffusion of water-soluble gases. Conifers and small-leaved deciduous trees have a particularly large leaf surface area. In a study of four American cities, New York, Philadelphia, Baltimore and Boston, with a tree cover of 16.6%, 21.6%, 18.9% and 21.2%, respectively, total pollution removal was 1821, 1031, 499 and 278 t, respectively (Nowak and Dwyer, 2000).

Trees are good absorbers of sulphur dioxide (SO_2). In the Greenwood Community Forest near Nottingham it has been estimated that the woodland reduces concentrations of SO_2 and NO_2 in the air by 4–5% (Broadmeadow and Freer-Smith, 1996).

Provision of shade and shelter

Vegetation modifies exposure to sun and winds. In the shade, temperatures can be several degrees lower than in the open. In coastal sites tall boundary trees provide protection from sea winds and allow for the cultivation of less robust plants.

Vegetation can create a reduced demand for central heating or air conditioning. However, a study of scientific literature by UK consultants suggested that vegetation provided a 3% reduction in energy demand, much less than the reduction shown when double glazing or cavity blocks were used (Patch, 1998). In Madison, Wisconsin, it was estimated that energy costs for a residence with appropriately positioned trees were 4% less than where no trees were grown, but that inappropriately placed trees raised energy costs by 13% (McPherson, 1987, cited by Nowak and Dwyer, 2000).

Reduction of noise levels

Trees contribute to a reduction in noise pollution. Tests based on dense green woodland with tree heights from 6 to 12 m showed that a 300-m wide band reduced high-pitch sound by up to 35 dB. Depending on the species planted, sound levels can be reduced by 4–12 dB (Bradshaw *et al.*, 1995).

Habitat creation

Vegetation provides cover for nesting birds and animals. Particular tree species, such as *Salix* (willow) and *Quercus* (oak), provide food for hundreds of phytophagous insects. A woodland floor is home to many wild-flower species such as *Hyacanthoides* (bluebell) and *Digitalis* (foxglove).

Engineering

Control of soil moisture and soil erosion

The tree canopy protects soil from direct sunlight and heavy rain. Roots prevent soil from being washed away. Leaf litter and decayed matter are incorporated into the soil and improve its ability to absorb water. Soil moisture content is controlled by trees absorbing water through their roots and reducing water movement. Runoff from hard surface areas can be channelled to planted areas. Studies in Maryland, USA, have shown that the annual sediment yield from treeless urban areas was as much as 1000 times greater than that from wooded urban areas – 50,000 t per square mile, compared with 50 t per square mile.

Soil stabilization

Vegetation has a role in stabilizing slopes. Roots bind soil together and reduce erosion and soil movement (Coppin and Stiles, 1990). The practice of bioengineering using *Salix* (willow) and *Populus* (poplar) is common by motorways and roads and along riverbanks. A tree canopy intercepts rainfall and stems, leaves and litter reduce the velocity of surface-water runoff.

Aesthetic Functions of Trees and Shrubs

Many features are appreciated and recognized by the general public as well as those with a professional interest in the subject. Trees and shrubs add colour and character to an area and highlight the changing seasons. The sound of wind in trees, shadows cast by a tracery of branches and the rustling sound of fallen autumn leaves catch many people's attention. Trees also make a visual contribution to their surroundings. In a survey undertaken in 66 English towns and villages, 79% of trees made a visual contribution to their surrounds and 21% did not. Street trees made a greater contribution than trees in parks or in private areas. The bigger and more imposing a tree the greater is its contribution (Land Use Consultants, 1993).

Trees provide a sense of identification with a locality, Derry, for example, from *dair*, the Gaelic for *Quercus* (oak), a city in Northern Ireland; Poplar, a suburb in east London, or Unter den Linden, a city centre street in Berlin where people have strolled beneath *Tilia* (lime or linden) trees since the 17th century.

In the USA, Ulrich *et al.* (1991) suggested that greenery and nature accelerated a person's recovery from stress. Patrik Grahn and Ulrika Stigsdotter (2003) described a study where they interviewed 953 individuals in nine Swedish cities and their results suggest that the more often a person visits an urban green space the less often they will report a stress-related illness.

Detrimental Effects of Vegetation in Urban Areas

While the beneficial effects of vegetation have been discussed, a number of detrimental effects are attributed to trees. The roots of trees are often alleged to cause damage to buildings and their foundations and to damage drains, but Gasson and Cutler (1998) conclude that with an appropriate distance between trees and buildings little conflict should occur. In 1986, of 2232 street trees surveyed (13% of the total) in Manchester, 30% and 13% were causing damage to pavements and kerbs, respectively (Wong *et al.*, 1988). Trees can obstruct light falling on a window and reduce the energy efficiency of a building, though light attenuation varies with tree species (Yates and McKennan, 1988).

Further investigation

Suggestion 1

Examine the use of vegetation in such places as a local park, shopping centre, housing estate, traffic intersection or campus. Describe the function of each scheme and illustrate where appropriate. Look in particular for linkage, space dividers, barrier planting, camouflage and soil stabilization. How successful is the use of vegetation for the particular function?

Suggestion 2

Prepare a table similar to Table 1.1, naming particular schemes and noting the design, engineering, environmental and aesthetic function(s) of each.

Table 1.1. Investigation of functional uses of vegetation in a locality.

Type of scheme	Design	Engineering	Environmental	Aesthetic
River walk in village	Linked with other waterways	Stabilization of riverbank with *Salix* (willow)	Wildlife – I glimpsed a kingfisher	
Supermarket car park	Unity demonstrated by lines of trees on the site		Shade for cars	Attractive autumn colour
Canal walk in rural area				

References

Anon. (1999) Carbon storage in Edinburgh. *Landlines* 102, August 1999.
Bradshaw, A., Hunt, B. and Walmsley, T. (1995) *Trees in the Urban Landscape: Principles and Practice*. E. and F.N. Spon, London.

Broadmeadow, M. and Freer-Smith, P. (1996) *Urban Woodland and the Benefits for Local Air Quality.* HMSO, London.

Coppin, N. and Stiles, R. (1990) The use of vegetation in slope stabilization. In: Clouston, B. (ed.) *Landscape Design with Plants.* Butterworth Architecture, Oxford, UK, pp. 212–234.

Gasson, P.E. and Cutler, D.F. (1998) Can we live with trees in our towns and cities? *Arboricultural Journal* 22, 1–9.

Grahn, P. and Stigsdotter, U.A. (2003) Landscape planning and stress. *Urban Forestry and Urban Greening* 2, 1–18.

Innes, J.L. (1990) Plants and air pollution. In: Clouston, B. (ed.) *Landscape Design with Plants.* Butterworth Architecture, Oxford, UK, pp. 199–211.

Land Use Consultants (1993) *Trees in Towns: A Survey of Trees in 66 Towns and Villages in England.* Research for Amenity Trees No.1, HMSO, London.

Nowak, D.J. (1993) Atmospheric carbon reduction by urban trees. *Journal of Environmental Management* 37, 207–217.

Nowak, D.J. and Dwyer J.F. (2000) Understanding the benefits and costs of urban forest ecosystems. In: Kuser, J.E. (ed.) *Handbook of Urban and Community Forestry in the Northeast.* Kluwer Academic/Plenum Publishers, New York, pp. 11–25.

Patch, D. (1998) *Trees, Shelter and Energy Conservation.* Arboricultural Research Note 145/Arb/98, DOE Arboricultural Advisory and Information Service, Farnham, UK.

Ulrich, R.S., Simons, R.F., Losito, B.D., Fiorito, E., Miles, M.A. and Zelson, M. (1991) Stress recovery during exposure to natural and urban environments. *Journal of Environmnental Psychology* 11, 201–230.

Wong, T.W., Good, J.E.G. and Denne, M.P. (1988) Tree root damage to pavements and kerbs in the city of Manchester. *Arboricultural Journal* 12, 17–34.

Yates, D. and McKennan, G. (1988) Solar architecture and light attenuation by trees: conflict or compromise? *Landscape Research* 13(1), 19–23.

2 Ornamental Qualities of Trees and Shrubs

A walk in a park brings the ornamental or decorative qualities of trees and shrubs to life. Compare the sheer size of a *Quercus* (oak) and the grandeur of a *Fraxinus excelsior* 'Pendula' (weeping ash) with the delicate green leaves of young foliage on *Salix sepulcralis* var. *chrysocoma* (weeping willow). Contrast the chartreuse green flowers of *Acer pseudoplatanus* (sycamore) and the bright pink of some flowering *Prunus* (cherries). In autumn, brown conkers of *Aesculus* (horse chestnut) and dark red fruits of *Sorbus* (rowan) attract the attention of passers-by. Winter light shows the bark of *Betula* (birch) in almost brilliant white.

When designing with plants, a knowledge of the individual characteristics of trees and shrubs is a prerequisite for success. The growth rate, longevity or lifespan and the shape of the tree or shrubs need to be considered when grouping trees or shrubs in planting schemes. Similarly, when maintaining plant schemes, the changing quality of plants over the season or the dynamic quality of a scheme must be borne in mind. Some trees come into leaf early in the year, while others leaf out later but hold their leaves until late autumn. Some shrubs flower or fruit in their early years, while others require a period of time before they commence to flower and fruit.

Growth Rate

Some genera take a few years to become established and then their growth rate increases, while others grow quickly in the initial years and then their growth rate slows down. Some trees and shrubs are fast-growing and short-lived, *Betula* (birch) and *Alnus* (alder), for example, live for 40–50 years, whereas oak (*Quercus*) is slow-growing and lives for some 200 years. Growth rate is also affected by the mode of spread of a species, its competitiveness and ability to withstand soil, climate and cultural conditions.

© M. Forrest 2006. *Landscape Trees and Shrubs: Selection, Use and Management* (M. Forrest)

Plant Size

Tree and shrub sizes vary and a general guide to trees and shrubs in the categories of small, medium and large is given in Table 2.1. Eventual plant size varies among genera; for instance, *Fagus sylvatica* (beech) becomes a large tree, while trees from the genus *Malus* (crab apple) are usually small- to medium-sized trees. The contrast in the sizes of mature trees is seen in Fig. 2.1. Plant size can also vary greatly even within the same genus – for example, a small ornamental *Acer palmatum* (Japanese maple) in contrast to a 35-m tall *Acer macrophyllum* (Oregon maple). Similarly, within *Cotoneaster*, a genus of shrubs common in the landscape trade, *C. dammeri*, a wide-spreading, ground-hugging shrub, contrasts with the 5-m tall tree-like *C. lacteus*.

Shape

Trees by virtue of their size and longevity play a dominant role in the appearance of a landscape in a rural or urban area and these trees have a

Table 2.1. Heights of trees and shrubs

Trees		Shrubs	
Small	2–10 m	Small	30–100 cm
Medium	11–20 m	Medium	100–200 cm
Large	> 20 m	Large	> 200 cm

Fig. 2.1. Contrasting sizes of mature trees, small *Malus* (crab apple) in the foreground and tall *Fagus sylvatica* (beech) on the skyline.

particular shape or form. The shape or form of the tree is the outline it presents on or against the skyline. If the natural landscape is considered, some shapes dominate in a particular region.

In the natural landscape of much of England and Ireland, a rounded outline of trees occurs, e.g. large woodlands of *Fagus* (beech) and *Quercus* (oak) (Fig. 2.2). In Mediterranean regions, upright, conical *Cupressus sempervirens* (Italian cypress) and wide, dome-shaped *Pinus halepensis* (Aleppo pine) and *Pinus pinea* (stone pine) dominate the landscape.

Shape will vary depending on whether a tree is free-standing, in a group or in a woodland. This is especially the case with large parkland trees. The shape of a tree may change over its lifetime. As young trees, *Tilia* (lime) are broadly triangular in outline and, as they mature, they develop into large, dome-shaped trees. *Pinus sylvestris* (Scots pine) remains a bushy tree for many years; as it matures, the bushy form disappears to reveal a number of tall, upright trunks, with a distinctive orange bark.

1. Rounded outline, e.g. *Fagus* (beech). This shape of tree is used where there is plenty of space for the tree to grow and develop (Fig. 2.3). It is often seen in parkland schemes. Variations on the rounded theme include:
a. Globular *Acer platanoides* 'Globosum' (a form of Norway maple with a flattened head). It is often used where space is limited and a more 'constricted' shape is required in a formal layout.
b. Dome-like *Robinia pseudoacacia* 'Umbraculifera', a form of honey locust with a dense, round head. It is also used where space is limited and a more

Fig. 2.2. 400-year-old *Quercus* (oak) in Ashtown Wood, Phoenix Park, Dublin.

Fig. 2.3. Rounded outline of a mature *Fagus* (beech) tree.

Fig. 2.4. Umbrella-shaped mature *Pinus sylvestris* (Scots pine).

'constricted' shape is required in a formal layout.

c. Umbrella shape in later life of conifers, e.g. *P. pinea* (stone pine) or *P. sylvestris* (Scots pine) (Fig. 2.4).

d. Lollipop shape, e.g. *Sorbus aucuparia* 'Sheerwater Seedling' and *Sorbus x thuriangiaca* 'Fastigiata' (Fig. 2.5) (both forms of rowan), used as street trees because of their shape. Vehicles and pedestrians can pass beneath or to the side of such trees.

e. Vase shape, e.g. *Sorbus* 'Joseph Rock' (form of rowan), used as street trees because of the shape.

2. *Conical.* This shape is common in conifers, especially when they are younger, *Picea omorika* (Serbian spruce) being one the best examples (Fig. 2.6). Among the broadleaved trees, many *Populus* (poplar) have a conical shape, though it is not as pronounced as in some of the coniferous species (Fig. 2.7).

3. *Columnar.* As the name suggests, a column-like shape. They are sometimes used as 'exclamation points' or where space is limited between tall buildings. This shape is also used to close a view, as in St Catherine's College in Oxford in the design by Arne Jacobsen. *Prunus serrulata* 'Amanogawa' (an upright form of Japanese cherry), *Cupressus sempervirens* (Italian cypress) and *Populus nigra* 'Italica' (Lombardy poplar) are other examples (Fig. 2.8).

4. *Cylindrical* is similar in shape but over years the tree becomes broader. An example is *Taxus baccata* 'Fastigiata' (Irish yew), often seen in graveyards (Fig. 2.9).

Habit

Habit refers to the branching pattern of a tree or shrub. On deciduous plants the habit is best seen in winter, when the branches and the manner in which they are held on the plant are very evident (Fig. 2.10). Branching density is also apparent

Fig. 2.5. Lollipop-shaped tree, *Sorbus x thuriangiaca* 'Fastigiata' (rowan).

Fig. 2.7. *Populus × canadensis* 'Robusta' with a backdrop of small dome-shaped trees.

Fig. 2.6. Conical outline of a mature *Picea omorika* (Serbian spruce).

Fig. 2.8. Columnar shape of *Populus nigra* 'Italica' (Lombardy poplar) formed by fastigiate or vertical-growing branches.

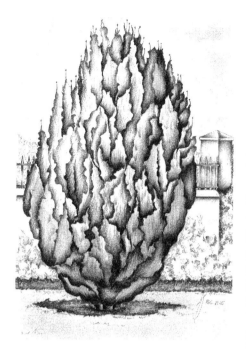

Fig. 2.9. Cylindrical shape of *Taxus baccata* 'Fastigiata' (Irish yew).

in winter. *Carpinus betulus* 'Fastigiata' is densely branched, whereas *Quercus robur* (oak) has a more open branching pattern.

Where the branching pattern is composed of many thin shoots and stems, for example, *Salix* (willow) and *Betula* (birch), even out of leaf it will act as a screen. This is in contrast to trees such as *Aesculus hippocastanum* (horse chestnut), which has thick shoots and buds but can look sparse and bare in winter. Types of habit include:

1. Regular. Described as a pattern of branches with a wide angle between the main trunk and the lower branches and narrower angles between the upper branches and the main trunk. Examples include the parkland trees *Fagus* (beech), *Tilia* (lime) and *Quercus* (oak) and *Morus nigra* (mulberry), a medium-sized, long-lived tree (Fig. 2.11).

2. Upright. Described as branches inclined upwards with a narrow angle between side branches and main stem. Some common examples among trees in present-day landscapes are *Betula utilis* var. *jacquemontii* (a white-stemmed birch), *Corylus colurna* (Turkish hazel), several hybrid *Ulmus* (elm) (Fig. 1.2) and *Acer platanoides* 'Deborah' (Fig. 2.12).

3. Pendulous. Branches that hang downwards are known as pendulous or weeping. They are often used as specimen trees, as too many together in a scheme can be overpowering. Some pendulous trees can be large, up to 30 m, *Fagus sylvatica* 'Pendula' (weeping beech) and *Fraxinus excelsior* 'Pendula' (weeping ash) (Fig. 2.13) being the largest growing. Some are medium-sized, such as *Pyrus salicifolia* 'Pendula' (weeping pear) and *Betula pendula* 'Youngii' (weeping birch), while others are small, such as dwarf willow, *Salix caprea* 'Kilmarnock', and *Prunus pendula* 'Pendula Rosea', which are therefore suitable for smaller areas.

4. Semi-pendulous. Semi-pendulous branches occur on two commonly planted species in rural areas, a deciduous conifer, *Larix decidua* (larch) (Fig. 2.14), and *Betula pendula* (birch).

5. Horizontal. A small number of trees and shrubs have a more or less horizontal branching habit. Examples among the trees are *Prunus* 'Shirotae', *Prunus* 'Taihaku' (both Japanese cherries), *Cornus controversa* (cornelian cherry) and *C. controvesa* 'Variegata' and among the shrubs *Viburnum plicatum*. These shapes are used as specimen trees and may be grouped to create archways and natural walkways in places such as shopping centres or hospital grounds or to link with a horizontal pattern of a wall or building.

Fig. 2.10. Habit or branching pattern of *Crataegus* (hawthorn) in winter with the branches clearly visible.

Fig. 2.11. Mature specimen of *Morus nigra* (mulberry) showing a regular branching pattern.

6. Fastigiate. A fastigiate branching pattern occurs where stems grow almost vertically upwards. Examples include *Populus nigra* 'Italica' (Lombardy poplar) (Fig. 2.8), *Taxus baccata* 'Fastigiata' (Fig. 2.9), *Prunus* 'Amanogawa', a Japanese cherry, *Fagus sylvatica* 'Dawyck' (Dawyck beech) and *Quercus robur* 'Fastigiata', an oak commonly planted as a landscape tree in recent years. These trees retain a columnar-like shape into maturity. A commonly planted hornbeam in urban areas, *Carpinus betulus* 'Fastigiata', despite its name has upright stems as a young tree but they become fan-shaped as the tree matures and the overall shape is more like a lollipop.

7. Mat-like. Many shrubs have a mat-like, prostrate or spreading growth habit (Fig. 2.15). Common examples are the native *Juniperus communis* (juniper) and the

Fig. 2.12. Upward-growing branches of *Acer platanoides* 'Deborah'.

landscape ground-cover shrubs *Rubus tricolor* and *Cotoneaster dammeri*. Such plants are useful for ground cover as they will grow one into another and form effective weed smother, whereas a dome-shaped shrub will remain within its shape and can allow infestations of weeds to develop between dome-shaped shrubs.

Types of Foliage

Deciduous trees and shrubs lose their leaves in autumn. Evergreen leaves are shed but on an infrequent basis, often in the spring of the year when new leaves emerge or are often held for a number of years. Depending on the season the character of a tree can differ (Fig. 2.16).

Leaves vary in size from tiny leaves of a few millimetres, e.g. *Cupressus* (cypress), to large leaves up to those of *Catalpa*

Fig. 2.13. Pendulous or weeping habit of *Fraxinus excelsior* 'Pendula' (weeping ash).

Fig. 2.14. Semi-pendulous habit of *Larix decidua* (larch).

Fig. 2.15. Mat-like or spreading growth habit of a conifer in association with conical-shaped conifers.

(Indian bean tree), 25 cm long by 20 cm broad on young shoots. Trees with large leaves and a many-branched crown, such as *Aesculus* (horse chestnut) and *Platanus* (plane), cast a lot of shade and plant establishment beneath mature trees of such species can be difficult. Some leaves have noticeable venation, e.g. *Viburnum davidii*, while some are glossy, including *Prunus laurocerasus* (cherry laurel), *Prunus lusitanica* (Portugese laurel) and *Camellia*, which are frequently grown examples. Some leaves are soft to the touch, e.g. *Phlomis* (Jerusalem sage), while others, such as *Berberis* (barberry) and *Ilex* (holly), are edged in tiny spines. Scent is an important feature of some leaves, such as *Lavandula* (lavender), *Rosmarinus* (rosemary) and *Laurus nobilis* (bay laurel), which are well-known ornamental shrubs and also culinary herbs.

The texture of foliage can vary greatly and this is seen especially in pinnate-leaved species. For example, the filigree effect of pinnate leaves on *Acacia* and some small-leaved rowan, e.g. *Sorbus vilmorinii*, contrasts with the large, coarsely textured, palmate foliage of *Aesculus* (horse chestnut). While most leaves are some shade of green, purple, glaucous (bluish) and variegated leaves occur. Variegation is seen in combinations of green and yellow, green and silver and purple and pale pink.

Some trees and shrubs produce attractive young foliage, particularly, for example, *Pieris* and *Photinia*, both with young red leaves. Autumn colour is particularly prominent among the *Acer* (maple) and *Hamamelis* (witch hazel) genera.

Flowers and Fruit

These can provide seasonal interest. Whatever the time of year, it is usually possible to find some flower or fruit, or

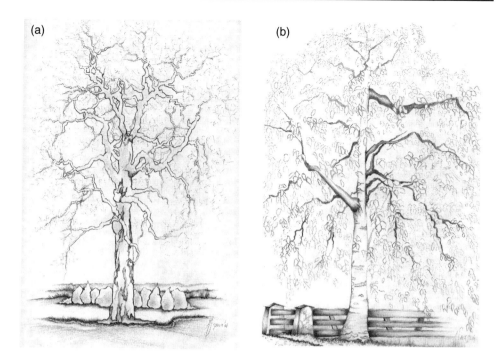

Fig. 2.16. Note the different character of a tree in and out of leaf.

remnants of fruit in a local area, be it city or country. Flowers can be tiny and elusive, like the green flowers on the hedge plant *Griselinia*, or large, such as the goblet-shaped *Magnolia*. Colours vary from the bright yellow of *Forsythia*, the mauve of *Syringa* (lilac) to the many colours of roses. The scent of some flowers can be noticeable on the winter air, e.g. *Jasminum* (jasmine), or on a hot summer's day with the heavy scent of *Ulex europaeus* (gorse, furze or whin).

Fruits vary from small apples on a recently planted weeping *Malus* (Fig. 2.17) to orange berries of *Pyracantha*, beloved of birds in winter, to the red of holly (*Ilex*) at Christmas to the hard brown capsules of *Cupressus macrocarpa* (Monterey cypress).

Bark

While present through the year, the bark effect comes into its own in winter. Some bark is soft to the touch, for example, that of the conifer *Sequoiadendron giganteum* (giant redwood) which has soft cork-like bark. Orange peeling bark is noticeable on *Acer griseum* (paperbark maple) and *Prunus serrula* (a cherry) has mahogany-coloured bark (Fig. 2.18). White-coloured bark is a feature of many of the birches (*Betula*). Snake bark maples (*Acer*) are a group of maples grown for their attractive bark, smooth and green with conspicuous white stripes. Among the parkland trees, old specimens of

Castanea sativa (sweet chestnut) are recognizable at a distance for their spirals of heavy ridges on the trunk and so are *Pseudotsuga menziesii* (Douglas fir) with their deeply fissured bark.

Further Investigation

Suggestion 1

A local park, shopping centre, business park, historic estate or suburban residential area is rarely tree- or shrubless. Identify examples of the following and sketch where appropriate:

    Shape/form
    Habit
    Flowers
    Fruit
    Foliage
    Bark effect

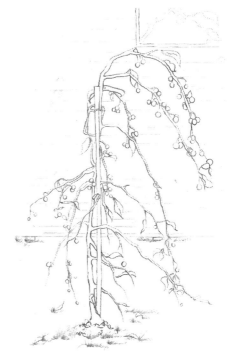

Fig. 2.17. Fruit on a newly planted *Malus* (crab apple).

Fig. 2.18. *Prunus serrula* has a mahogany-coloured bark and distinctive bands of lenticels.

Suggestion 2

Select a number of trees and shrubs with which you are familiar and complete Table 2.2. Three examples are completed in the table.

Table 2.2. Complete the following table with examples of trees in the local area.

Name	*Betula pendula*	*Aesculus hippocastanum*	*Taxus baccata*
Common name	Birch	Horse chestnut	English yew
Height	To 10–15 m	To 25 m	8–10 m
Shape	Rounded	Rounded, tall, statuesque	Broadly dome-shaped
Habit	Many thin branches	Thick shoots and branches	Wide-spreading
Leaves	Deciduous	Deciduous	Evergreen
Leaf shape	Elliptic	Palmate	Linear
Flower	Green catkins	White candle-like	Male yellow pollen
Fruit	Catkins	Conkers	Red aril
Bark	White	Brown	Fluted trunk
Autumn colour	Some years	Poor	None

Further Reading

Booth, N.K. (1983) *Basic Elements of Landscape Architectural Design.* Elsevier, New York.
Crowe, S. (1999) *Garden Design,* 3rd edn. Garden Art Press, Woodbridge, UK.
Trowbridge, P.J. and Bassuk, N.L. (2004) *Trees in the Urban Landscape: Site Assessment, Design, and Installation,* Wiley, Hoboken, New Jersey.

3   Plant Identification – an Introduction

Anyone visiting a public or academic library will notice that books on a particular subject are classified with a common number and placed together on shelves or stacks. In a similar way plants and animals are classified and have been given scientific names, a subject known as taxonomy.

The beginnings of plant nomenclature are attributed to the Greek botanist Theophrastus (372–287 BC). In the 18th century the Swedish botanist Carl Linné (Linnaeus) (1702–1778) established the system of binomial nomenclature, where each plant is given two names. These two names are genus (plural genera) and species. (In human terms the genus is akin to a person's family name and the species to their forename.) Botanists arranged genera into families and then into orders, subclasses and classes (Table 3.1).

Botanical Classification

Class

The class *Angiospermae* refers to the angiosperms or flowering plants and the class *Gymnospermae* to the gymnosperms or conifers. A comparative study of their flowers and fruits is the basis for the classification of higher plants. In the *Gymnospermae*, from the Greek *gymnos*, 'naked', and *spermae*, 'seed', the seed is naked, i.e. not enclosed in a seed case. Take a ripe pine cone, for example: the seeds are visible among the cone scales. In the *Angiospermae*, from the Greek *aggeion*, a vessel, and *spermae*, 'seed', the seed is enclosed in a seed case. *Aesculus* (horse chestnut) and *Malus* (apple) are examples. One subclass of the class of *Angiospermae*, is the *Dicotyledoneae*, commonly called dicotyledons, because on germination two cotyledons (seed leaves) develop. The other subclass of the *Angiospermae*, *Monocotyledoneae*,

© M. Forrest 2006. *Landscape Trees and Shrubs: Selection, Use and Management* (M. Forrest)

WARWICKSHIRE COLLEGE LIBRARY

Table 3.1. Classification of plant names.

Category	Scientific name	Scientific name
Class	*Angiospermae*	*Gymnospermae*
Subclass	*Dicotyledoneae*	
Order	*Fagales*[a]	*Coniferales*
Family	*Fagaceae*[b]	*Pinaceae*
Genus	*Fagus*	*Cedrus*
Species	*sylvatica*	*atlantica*
Authority	L.	(Endlicher) Carrière
Subspecies		
Varietas	e.g. *heterophylla*	
Forma	e.g. f. *laciniata*	
Cultivar	e.g. 'Dawyck'	e.g. 'Glauca Pendula'
Common name	Beech	Cedar

[a] A word ending in *ales* indicates an order. [b] A word ending in *aceae* indicates a family.

commonly referred to as monocots, with one cotyledon (seed leaf), include many of the bulbous plants and are not dealt with in this book.

Order

Orders refer to groups of families, which botanists recognize as having a number of common features. The rank of 'order' is designated by the letters '*ales*'.

Family

Family refers to a group of genera that have been grouped together. There are a number of families that contain one genus with one species (monotypic), e.g. *Ginkgoaceae*, *Ginkgo biloba*, and/or one genus, e.g. *Hippocastanaceae*, *Aesculus*. The rank of family is designated by the letters '*aceae*'.

Genus

Genus (plural genera) refers to a group of plants that are similar in flower and fruit, e.g. *Malus* (crab apple) or *Pinus* (pine). The genus name is written in italics with the first letter in upper case and the remaining letters lower case.

Species

Plants that hold a great similarity to one another are included in the same species.

The species name is written in italics in lower case, e.g. *palmatum*.

There are a number of classifications below species level which occur in the wild, namely, subspecies, varietas (abbreviated to var.) and forma. Examples are *Hydrangea anomala* subsp. *petiolaris* and *Fagus sylvatica* var. *heterophylla.*

Authority

The person who first validly published a botanical description of a plant is known as the authority for that particular plant. For example, Linnaeus, sometimes shortened to L followed by a full stop. Where one botanist names a plant and another botanist, having undertaken further examination of the genus, publishes a second description, then both names are given. An example of this is shown in Table 3.1. When a plant is described what is known as a 'type specimen' is deposited in a herbarium, where it can be consulted by other botanists. Duplicate specimens may then be sent to other herbaria.

Cultivar

Cultivar refers to variations that have been selected in cultivation or in the wild and which have been vegetatively propagated by gardeners. *Fagus sylvatica* 'Dawyck', listed in Table 3.1, is named for the garden at Dawyck, near Edinburgh, Scotland. A cultivar name is written with a prefix 'cv.' before the name or with a single quotation mark either side of the name. As an example of cultivar names of importance to a landscape designer, *Aucuba japonica* has green leaves but the plant named *A. japonica* 'Variegata' has mottled yellow foliage, so that selecting one would create a green coloured scheme and the other a yellow scheme. A group of 20 *Fraxinus excelsior* (ash) in a scheme will create a very different effect from that of a group of *F. excelsior* 'Pendula' (weeping ash).

Some species hybridize in the wild, but most of those used as landscape trees and shrubs have been the deliberate work of nurserymen and plant breeders. Hybrids are denoted by a × before the species name, e.g. *Abelia × grandiflora*, or before the genus name in the case of a hybrid between genera, e.g. × *Cupressocyparis leylandii.*

Common or Colloquial Names

Many plants have common names. This is especially the case with native trees and shrubs, e.g. *Crataegus*, commonly called hawthorn, quickthorn, thornquick or maybush. A common name is often localized. In Ireland, for instance whin, gorse and furze are common names for one shrub, *Ulex europaeus*. Given that it is native to Europe, it must have a great many common names across the continent. What is called lime in Britain and Ireland is linden or basswood in the USA, these common names referring to one genus, *Tilia*. A common name can also refer to a number of genera. Those living in coastal areas will know a tree with a single trunk and strap-like foliage as a palm tree – *Cordyline australis*. However, further inland, dark evergreen trees often used to screen houses are also known as palm trees, referring to *Taxus baccata, Chamaecyparis lawsoniana* or × *Cupressocyparis leylandii*.

Scientific names are generally derived from Latin and Greek, for example, *Rhododendron, Rhodo,* rose, and *dendron,* tree, in Greek, or from a Latinized form of some language, for example, *Magnolia grandiflora* named for a French botanist, Pierre Magnol, and *grandiflora,* large flower. Cultivar names are derived from various sources. Some are Latinized forms of English (e.g. *Euonymus japonicus* 'Variegata'), some have attractive commercial names such as *Choisya ternata* 'Sundance', while others are named for a garden or nursery where the plant was raised e.g. *Solanum crispum* 'Glasnevin'.

Why do Plant Names Change?

Further examination of plant specimens, in herbaria, in the wild or as a result of DNA analysis, provides botanists with new information about plant identification and a revision of plant names ensues. Some plant names revert to an older name, e.g. *Viburnum fragrans* is now known as *Viburnum farreri,* while others are 'sunk', combined in other species, e.g. *Hydrangea petiolaris* is now *H. anomala* var. *petiolaris*.

Plant nomenclature is regulated by the International Code of Botanical Nomenclature (Greuter *et al.,* 2000) and the International Code for Nomenclature for Cultivated Plants (Brickell *et al.,* 2004). The former deals with 'wild plants', which may occur in the wild or may be cultivated, and the latter deals with 'cultivars', which are also cultivated.

In this book, family names and names of genera are taken from the *Handbook of North European Garden Plants* (Cullen, 2001) and species names and names below the species classification are taken from the *RHS Plant Finder 2005–2006* (Lord, 2005).

What's in a Name

The editors of the *RHS Plant Finder 2005–2006* quote W.J. Bean from his preface for the first edition of *Trees and Shrubs Hardy in the British Isles.* 'The question of nomenclature is always a vexed one. The only thing certain is that it is impossible to please everyone.' First published in 1914, Bean's comment still holds true and his comprehensive treatment of trees and shrubs, now in its eighth edition, remains a classic.

While plant names are necessary in landscape design and in horticulture so that correct plant selection or plant management can be undertaken, the words of Romeo to Juliet in Shakespeare's *Romeo and Juliet,* 'What's in a name? that which we call a rose/By any other name would smell as sweet,' are a reminder that a plant is more than the name it has been given. However, plant names can assist the landscape designer or horticulturist in plant selection and management and be an aide-memoire in plant identification.

An explanation of plant names is given in Stearn (1992). Scientific names of plants can sometimes give a clue to the use of a plant in design or to its cultural requirements. Some words refer to the habit or form of a plant, e.g. *repens*, creeping, or *fastigiata* upright-growing habit; the latter would never be a suitable ground-cover plant. Other names provide a clue to cultivation requirements; *sylvatica* indicates a woodland or shaded habitat.

The country of origin can be helpful. Plants with the specific names of *chinensis* and *japonica* are widely cultivated in Western Europe. Caution would have to be exercised when selecting plants with the specific names of *hispanica* or *lusitanica*, indicating plants from Spain and Portugal with a more Mediterranean climate than in north-western Europe. They would be suitable for the milder rather than the colder regions of Britain and Ireland.

Many plant names give an indication of leaf and flower type and can be a useful tool for a person checking a delivery from a nursery. A consignment of plants with the specific name of *microphylla* ought to have a small leaf and a plant with the specific name of *alternifolia* would have alternate rather than opposite foliage.

While some names do not provide any clue to cultivation or identification, they provide a link with previous generations of plant collectors, plant breeders and nurseries.

Geographical

Aucuba japonica	Japan
Sorbus hupehensis	Hubei, a region in western China
Genista hispanica	Spain
Thuja orientalis	the Orient
Ulex europaeus	Europe
Prunus lusitanica	Portugal
Carpenteria californica	California
Acer cappadocicum	Cappadocia (Turkey)

Habitat – clue to cultivation

Fagus sylvatica	woodland
Pinus sylvestris	woodland
Acer campestre	of the field
Griselinia littoralis	seashore
Pinus nigra var. *maritima*	maritime

Habit – shape/outline

Ceanothus thyrsiflorus var. *repens*	creeping or spreading
Rosmarinus officinalis prostratus group	prostrate or spreading

Taxus baccata 'Fastigiata'	fastigiate/upright growth habit
Betula pendula	weeping or pendulous habit
Cotoneaster horizontalis	horizontal branching habit
Lupinus arboreus	tree-like
Potentilla fruticosa	shrubby
Teucrium fruticans	shrubby

Leaves

phylla (um) (us) *folia* (um) (us)	leaf
Buddleja alternifolia	alternate leaves
Lavandula angustifolia	narrow leaves
Rosa glauca	glaucous leaves – a bluish-grey colour
Acer palmatum	palmate or hand-shaped
A. palmatum Dissectum Atropurpureum Group	palmate foliage is dissected or finely cut and deep purple in colour
Rosa rugosa	leaves puckered
Prunus serrula	margins of leaves serrated like the teeth on a small saw
Prunus serrulata	margins of the leaves serrated with tiny saw-like teeth
Cotoneaster microphyllus	small leaves
Acer macrophyllum	large leaves
Choisya ternata	foliage in clusters of three
Aucuba japonica 'Variegata'	variegated foliage
Ligustrum ovalifolium	oval foliage
Buxus sempervirens	evergreen
Betula pubescens	hairs on the young shoots

Names alluding to other plants

Pterocarya fraxinifolia	*Ptero* (false), *Carya* (hickory), *fraxinifolia*, foliage like *Fraxinus* (ash)
Robinia pseudoacacia	foliage like that of *Acacia*
Carpinus betulus	foliage like that of *Betula* (birch)
Hydrangea quercifolia	foliage like that of *Quercus* (oak)
Ribes laurifolium	leaves shaped like *Laurus nobilis* (bay laurel)
Pyrus salicifolia cv Pendula	a willow-leaved, pendulous *Pyrus* (pear)

Scents and aromas

Lavandula officinalis	plants with real or imagined medicinal properties, many are scented
Ribes odoratus	scented

Flowers

Magnolia grandiflora	large flowers
Magnolia stellata	flowers stellate, star-like from the Latin *stella*, star
Liriodendron tulipifera	flowers like that of a tulip
Hydrangea paniculata	flowers in a panicle

Seed and fruit

Cupressus macrocarpa	large seed

Names that are commemorative

Parthenocissus henryana was named for Augustine Henry (1857–1930), a plant collector in China and later Professor of Forestry in University College, Dublin.

Sorbus sargentiana was named for Charles Sprague Sargent (1841–1927), Director of the Arnold Arboretum of Harvard University, Cambridge, Massachusetts, USA. With no other basis than serendipity, plants that bear the name of Sargent are worth a search in specialist nurseries for cultivation in well-favoured landscape situations, e.g. *Hydrangea aspera* subsp. *sargentiana, Malus toringo* var. *sargentii, Prunus sargentii, Magnolia sargentiana* and *Viburnum sargentii*.

Magnolia x soulangeana commemorates two French people: Pierre Magnol (1638–1715), Professor of Botany at Montpellier and Etienne Soulange-Bodin (1774–1846), a horticulturist from Fromont near Paris, who raised this hybrid magnolia.

Philadelphus x lemoinii recalls Lemoine, a father and son of Nancy, France, who in the 19th century raised hybrids of shrubby species, including *Philadelphus* and *Deutzia*.

Scheme for the Identification and Use of Plants by Family

The schema for the identification, use and management of each family described in Chapter 4 is as follows.

Family name

For example, *Rosaceae*. Brief description of the family, in terms of its identification or value in a landscape scheme.

Types of plants

Trees, shrubs, climbers, herbaceous perennials, annuals. Some families have a range of plant types (e.g. *Rosaceae*), while others are primarily trees (*Betulaceae*, birch family) or shrubs (*Caprifoliaceae*, elderberry family).

World distribution

This can have a bearing on where the plants can be cultivated, particularly in relation to climate. For instance, plants native to the Mediterranean region or Australia and New Zealand generally grow in well-favoured situations, often maritime regions of Ireland, south-west England and western Scotland.

Leaves

The type of foliage, e.g. opposite, alternate, pinnate, is often common to a particular family, e.g. *Acer* (*Aceraceae*) have opposite leaves.

Flowers

The type of flower or flower colour may predominate in a family. In *Asteraceae* (daisy family) flowers are radially symmetrical.

Fruit

This is noticeable in some families and an important ornamental feature as well as providing food for wildlife.

Bark

This is not usually a distinctive feature in a family, but is in some genera, e.g. *Pinus* (pine).

Growth rate and longevity

Some families of trees, especially parkland trees, are very long-lived, whereas many, predominantly families of shrubs, have a short- to medium-length lifespan.

Functional and ornamental uses

A number of examples of the general uses of members of the family are listed.

Growing conditions

Some genera from certain families can be described as being tough individuals suitable for an inhospitable site, while others are more tender and will require good growing conditions.

Management

Reference is made to the pruning requirements of the family and whether it is prone to pests and diseases.

Particular planting schemes or plant associations

Examples of planting schemes seen by the author are given. Readers are encouraged to seek out examples for themselves.

References

Bean, W.J. (1970–1988) *Trees and Shrubs Hardy in the British Isles*, 8th edn. John Murray, London.

Brickell, C., Baum B.R., Hetterschneid, W.L.A., Leslie, A.C., Mc Neill, J., Trehane, P., Vrugtman, F. and Wiersema, J.H. (eds) (2004) *International Code for Nomenclature for Cultivated Plants*, 7th edn. Acta Horticulturae 647, International Society for Horticultural Science, Leuven, Belgium.

Cullen, J. (2001) *Handbook of North European Garden Plants*. Cambridge University Press, Cambridge, UK.

Greuter, W., McNeill, J., Barrie, F.R., Burdet, H.-M., Demoulin, V., Filgueiras, T.S., Nicolson, D.H., Silva, P.C., Skog, J.E., Trehane, P., Turland, N.J. and Hawksworth, D.L. (2000) *International Code of Botanical Nomenclature (St Louis Code)*. Regnum Vegetabile 138, Koeltz Scientific Books, Köningstein.

Stearn, W.T. (1992) *Stearn's Dictionary of Plant Names for Gardeners*. Cassell, London.

4 Plant Families

Aceraceae Maple

These are important trees for general landscape use in streets, parks and open spaces and naturalistic schemes. Some species and cultivars have particular ornamental uses in landscape and garden situations (Table 4.1). Opposite leaves and winged seed distinguish this genus from other genera of trees.

TYPES OF PLANTS. Trees – small (1–5 m) to medium (5–15 m) to large (> 15 m) tall.

WORLD DISTRIBUTION. They are native to the northern temperate world:

North America: especially eastern USA and Canada, where these trees produce superb autumn (fall) colour, e.g. *Acer saccharum* (sugar maple).
China: *Acer davidii.*
Japan: *Acer palmatum* and *Acer japonicum.*
Europe: *Acer campestre* (field maple), *Acer platanoides* (Norway maple) and *Acer pseudoplatanus* (sycamore). *A. pseudoplatanus* has become naturalized in Britain and Ireland.

LEAVES. They are usually deciduous, opposite, simple, stalked, with three to 13 lobes, palmate, e.g. *A. palmatum* or pinnate, *Acer negundo* and *Acer griseum.* Leaf margins are entire or serrated (Fig. 4.1).

FLOWERS. Yellow to greenish white flowers are noticeable in spring, either as drooping racemes (e.g. *A. davidii*, a snake bark maple, and *A. pseudoplatanus*) or as terminal erect corymbs, e.g. *A. platanoides.* In *A. negundo* (ash-leaved maple), male and female flowers are borne on separate trees. Male flowers are prominent in March, when they appear before the leaves.

© M. Forrest 2006. *Landscape Trees and Shrubs: Selection, Use and Management* (M. Forrest)

Table 4.1. *Acer* (maple) commonly available in the trade and encountered in parks and open spaces.

Medium–large trees
   Acer macrophyllum   Oregon maple
   Acer cappadocicum   Cappadocian maple
   Acer platanoides   Norway maple
   A. platanoides 'Crimson King'
   A. platanoides 'Drummondii'
   Acer pseudoplatanus   Sycamore
   A. pseudoplatanus 'Atropurpureum'
   A. pseudoplatanus f. *variegatum*
   Acer saccharinum

Small–medium sized maples
   Acer campestre   Field maple
   Acer tartaricum var. *ginnala*   Amur maple
   Acer negundo   Ash-leafed maple
   Acer nikoense
   A. platanoides 'Globosum'
   A. pseudoplatanus 'Brilliantissimum'
   A. pseudoplatanus f. *variegatum* 'Simon Louis Freres'

Japanese maples
   Acer japonicum
   A. japonicum 'Aconitifolium'
   Acer palmatum
   A. palmatum f. *atropurpureum*
   A. palmatum var. *heptalobum* 'Osakazuki'
   A. palmatum var. *dissectum*
   A. palmatum Dissectum Atropurpureum Group
   A. palmatum 'Sango-kaku'
   Acer shirasawanum 'Aureum'

Snake bark maples
   Acer capillipes
   Acer davidii
   Acer pensylvanicum
   Acer rufinerve

Paper bark maple
   Acer griseum

FRUIT. Two single-seeded samaras, a seed with a 'wing' attached; commonly called helicopters or keys. They are held in stalked clusters or hang in pendulous racemes.

BARK. Notable bark is a feature of *A. griseum* (paper bark maple), with peeling brown stems. Snake bark maples have green, smooth bark with white striations. Commonly planted examples are *A. davidii*, *A. capillipes* and *A. rufinerve*.

Figure 4.1. (A) *Acer pseudoplatanus*, sycamore; (B) *Acer campestre*, field maple; (C) *Acer platanoides*, Norway maple. (From Savill, 1991.)

GROWTH RATE AND LONGEVITY. *A. pseudoplatanus* (sycamore) is fast-growing and lives for 100–200 years. Japanese maples are slow-growing and attain full size after 100 years or so.

FUNCTIONAL AND ORNAMENTAL USES.

Parkland trees	*A. pseudoplatanus, A. macrophyllum*
Street trees	*A. platanoides* 'Columnare'
Reclamation sites	*A. pseudoplatanus*
Naturalistic planting schemes	*A. campestre*
Hedges	*A. campestre*

Shrubberies	*Acer tartaricum* subsp. *ginnala, A. palmatum, A. japonicum*
Small spaces and patio planters	*A. palmatum* and *A. japonicum* cultivars
Autumn colour	*A. cappadocicum, A. palmatum*
Winter interest	*A. griseum, A. davidii* and *A. palmatum* 'Sango-kaku'

GROWING CONDITIONS. Rich, moist soil is required for most maples. *A. campestre* grows satisfactorily in a range of soils. *A. pseudoplatanus* and *A. platanoides* will grow in poorer conditions, often seen in streets and urban areas. *A. pseudoplatanus* can become invasive. They do not grow well in shade.

A. pseudoplatanus will withstand wind and salt spray. It is one of the few trees that will survive in the prevailing south-westerly wind on the west coast of Ireland.

Other maples require a somewhat sheltered situation. The foliage of the Japanese maples can be damaged by frost and by excessive sunlight.

MANAGEMENT. Some formative pruning may be required in the early years, but *Acer* requires little attention. Where cultivars and in particular variegated cultivars are grown, any green branches should be removed as they are more vigorous than variegated branches and will outgrow them. *A. pseudoplatanus* and *A. platanoides* cast heavy shade and some pruning may be required to facilitate the growth of a shrub layer.

PESTS AND DISEASES. *A. pseudoplatanus* can become infested with aphids. A disease, tar spot *Rhytisina acerinum* occurs on the leaves, noticeable in autumn, but no control measures are used. Powdery mildew *Phyllactinia* can 'whiten' the leaves of *A. platanoides* 'Crimson King' in autumn.

In some urban areas horse chestnut scale insect *Pulvinaria regalis* is becoming a problem on *A. platanoides*, causing unsightly white scales on the bark and young shoots and debilitating the tree.

PARTICULAR PLANTING SCHEMES OR PLANT ASSOCIATIONS. In Northern and Central Europe, along with *Tilia, Platanus* and *Aesculus, A. platanoides* and *A. pseudoplatanus* are the most commonly planted trees in streets and in parks and urban woodland (Saebø *et al.*, 2005).

A. platanoides 'Globosum' trees, planted in a broad grass margin, line a main road in Churchtown, a Dublin suburb. In central Leipzig (Germany), the cultivar is used as a boundary between a park area and urban pedestrian zone.

A. macrophyllum (Oregon maple): in Library Square, Trinity College, Dublin, two specimens, probably planted in the mid-19th century, have developed into two large, wide-spreading, dome-shaped trees, some 16-m tall.

A. saccharinum (Silver maple): specimens of multi-stemmed trees with a ground cover of *Hedera helix* (ivy) mark the approach to the main entrance of the Frederiksberg Campus of Royal Veterinary and Agricultural University (KVL), Copenhagen (Fig. 4.2).

Fig. 4.2. Feathered specimens of *Acer saccharinum* (silver maple) and a ground cover of *Hedera helix* (ivy) mark an entrance to the Royal Veterinary and Agricultural University, Copenhagen.

Aquifoliaceae Holly

When growing in isolation from other trees and shrubs, these become tall conical specimens becoming ragged in older age. More often they are seen as bushy trees or shrubs beneath taller trees. While a prickly leaf is an immediate clue to identification, an acrid-smelling shoot can often indicate an *Ilex*.

TYPES OF PLANTS. Trees: small to medium-sized.
Shrubs: small, medium or large evergreen shrubs.

WORLD DISTRIBUTION. Europe, Canary Islands and Azores, Japan, China, Himalaya. One species, *Ilex aquifolium*, is native in Britain and Ireland.

LEAVES. Foliage is evergreen. Most species and cultivars have spines on the extremities of the leaves. On young plants and on epicormic growth (sprouts from the base of the tree), foliage is spined. As the tree grows, foliage becomes entire and is no longer spiny.

FLOWERS. Male and female flowers are borne on separate trees. They are held in clusters in the axils of leaves. Both have small, conspicuous, white petals; male flowers are identified by the presence of anthers and females by the presence of a stigma.

FRUIT. Clusters of globose-shaped red fruits develop in late summer and are held over the winter months, providing food for birds.

BARK. This is whitish grey, often smooth and sometimes with wart-like growths on the trunk.

GROWTH RATE AND LONGEVITY. *Ilex* is slow-growing but long-lived.

FUNCTIONAL AND ORNAMENTAL USES.

Native and naturalistic schemes	*I. aquifolium*
Urban, shaded, air-polluted areas	*I. aquifolium*
Air pollution	*I. aquifolium*
Hedges	*I. aquifolium*
Ground-cover	*I. crenata* 'Convexa'
Large shrub	*I.* × *altaclerensis* 'Hodginsii'
Variegated evergreen shrubs	*I.* × *altaclerensis* 'Golden King',
	I. aquifolium 'Silver Queen'

GROWING CONDITIONS. Male and female trees. They grow in shade and are useful in exposed windy places.

MANAGEMENT. *Ilex* must be transplanted with care. If not purchased as 'root-balled' or container-grown, care should be taken not to disturb the roots. Soil falls away from the roots and plant establishment is difficult.

Ilex can be pruned and will regenerate quickly.

PARTICULAR PLANTING SCHEMES AND PLANT ASSOCIATIONS. Shrubbery schemes in 19th-century gardens and public parks.

Some hollies common in landscape schemes are as follows:

I. crenata 'Convexa': low-growing, spreading shrub, not to be confused with *Buxus sempervirens* 'Suffruticosa'.

I. × *altaclarensis* and many cultivars: 'Golden King' female cultivar, 'Hodginsii' and 'Lawsoniana'.

I. aquifolium and many cultivars: 'Ferox' (hedgehog holly); 'Golden Milkboy' and 'Silver Queen' male cultivar.

———————————————— • ————————————————

Araucariaceae Monkey Puzzle, Chile Pine

One species, *Araucaria araucana*, is cultivated. It is a dome-shaped tree, sometimes clothed to the ground with wide-spreading branches, which are upswept at the extremities. It was once frequently planted in conifer collections in estates and as specimen trees in suburban and rural gardens, and many examples occur in the British Isles.

TYPES OF PLANTS. Trees: large to 20–26 m tall.

WORLD DISTRIBUTION. Argentina and Chile.

BARK. The trunk is straight and cylindrical, with grey crinkled bark and noticeable scars where branches once existed.

LEAVES. Evergreen, dark green leaves encircle the shoots and branchlets. They are triangular in outline and sharply pointed at the apex.

FLOWERS. Male flowers are borne in clusters at the tips of shoots, female flowers are globular and solitary.

FRUIT. Large, round, spined fruits 15 cm across take 2 years to mature. At first glance, they are not unlike the vegetable globe artichoke, but are dark green as opposed to grey-green.

GROWTH RATE AND LONGEVITY. *Araucaria* are slow-growing, adding a whorl of branches each year or every 2 years.

FUNCTIONAL AND ORNAMENTAL USES. Avenue tree and specimen tree.

GROWING CONDITIONS. Long-lived, they are majestic trees and require sufficient space to grow and develop so that their shape and stature can be appreciated. Too often they are planted in a confined space.

MANAGEMENT. Provided they have been given adequate space, they require little attention.

PARTICULAR PLANTING SCHEMES AND PLANT ASSOCIATIONS. In Britain and Ireland, a single specimen or two specimens situated either side of a hall door is a frequent sight in gardens of the early to mid-20th century.

It was often part of the collection of conifers planted in the late 19th and early 20th century, when conifers were very popular in estate and villa gardens.

Spectacular avenues of *Araucaria araucana* occur at Woodstock, Inistioge, County Kilkenny, and Powerscourt, County Wicklow, both in Ireland.

In 1994 a relative of *Araucaria*, *Wollemia nobilis* (Wollemi pine) was discovered in the Wollemi National Park, in the Blue Mountains near Sydney (www.wollemipine.com).

Asteraceae (*Compositae*) Daisy

A daisy-like flower and a 'fluffy' seed head are clues to the identification of this family. It also includes plants cultivated as garden annuals and perennials, e.g. marigolds and asters, cut flowers and pot plants sold as chrysanthemums, vegetable crops, such as globe artichoke (*Cynara scolymus*) and lettuce (*Lactuca*), and wild flowers, examples being the daisy (*Bellis perennis*) and dandelion (*Taraxacum officinale*). The evergreen shrubs discussed below are very valuable in maritime areas. Some withstand full exposure to wind and others thrive in the shelter of their family members.

TYPES OF PLANTS. Shrubs: less than a metre tall to very large shrubs, 10 m, of tree-like habit.

WORLD DISTRIBUTION. One of the largest families of flowering plants (approx. 1500 genera) with a worldwide distribution. The shrubby genera treated here are native to Australia, Tasmania and New Zealand and to the Mediterranean.

LEAVES. Foliage is evergreen, green, often thick, felted above and/or below, hence useful for maritime areas. In *Ozothamnus*, the foliage is often narrow with the margins of the leaves rolled inwards; in *Santolina*, it is linear, grey and scented.

FLOWERS. Flowers are small, grouped into a head known as a capitula. The individual flowers are inconspicuous but a conspicuous petal (strictly a ray or ligule), distinguished as disc flowers and ray flowers by Cullen (2001), occurs on most species. These petals are numerous and arranged around the perimeter of the flower. They are usually white in *Olearia* or yellow in the genus *Brachyglottis*. In *Santolina* ray flowers are absent.

FRUIT. Each fruit is composed of numerous individual seeds (achene), each with a pappus (a ring of hairs that carry the wind-dispersed seed). The seeds are packed together and resemble a short mophead paintbrush. While not of ornamental interest, they are a useful clue to identification. Remnants of the seed head remain on the shrub for several weeks, providing a clue for identification to genus level.

GROWTH RATE AND LONGEVITY. *Olearia* are fast-growing shrubs of 10–20 years duration before they begin to 'break open'. The genera *Brachyglottis*, *Santolina* and *Helichrysum* establish quickly and are fast-growing. *Ozothamnus* is a slow-growing genus.

FUNCTIONAL AND ORNAMENTAL USES.

Shrubberies in maritime area	*Olearia, Brachyglottis*
Grey foliage borders and herb gardens	*Santolina, Helichrysum*
Barrier planting and hedges in maritime areas	*Olearia traversii, O. macrodonta* (see Table 4.2 for other *Olearia*)

Flowering shrubs   *Olearia* (several), *Brachyglottis*
                                          Dunedin Group 'Sunshine' and
                                          B. monroi

GROWING CONDITIONS. Suitable for maritime areas. They tend not to grow well where rainfall is high and drainage is poor.

MANAGEMENT. *Olearia* respond to pruning. After 5–10 years, *Brachyglottis, Santolina* and *Helichrysum* tend to become ungainly in habit and will respond to pruning but not to severe pruning. *Ozothamnus* is an attractive dome-shaped shrub, but it tends to 'break open' after 8–10 years and is difficult to rejuvenate.

PARTICULAR PLANTING SCHEMES OR PLANT ASSOCIATIONS. In Ireland, *Olearia traversii* and *O. macrodonta* form large hedges in gardens and caravan parks on the western and south-eastern seaboard.

Table 4.2. Common and uncommon *Olearia* (daisy bush) for maritime sites.

Name	Size (m)	Function	Foliage	Time of flowering	Flower
Olearia phlogopappa 'Combers Blue', 'Combers Pink'	1	Early summer flowering shrubs for a very sheltered site	Small, narrow, toothed, thinly textured leaves	May	White, blue, pink
Olearia 'Waikeriensis'	1–2	Evergreen flowering shrub	Lanceolate, greyish-green leaves	May–June	Clusters of white flowers clothe the bush
Olearia 'Henry Travers'	1–2	Evergreen flowering shrub for sheltered maritime areas	Lanceolate greyish leaves, unfurling silver	June	Large single flowers in shades of mauve and lilac
Olearia macrodonta	4–6	Barrier planting, large bushy shrub	Greyish-green holly-like	June–July	Many clusters of white flowers
Olearia traversii	5–7	Barrier planting, large tree-like shrub	Greyish-green leaves, smooth and entire	July	Pale green, not conspicuous
Olearia × *haastii*	2–3	Neat hedging, medium-sized shrub	Small, entire, stiff, green leaves	August	Many clusters of small white flowers
Olearia avicennifolia	3–4	Bushy shrub, hedge	Pointed green leaves, white beneath	August–September	Many clusters of white flowers
Olearia paniculata	5–10	Barrier planting, large tree-like shrub	Lime-green, leathery, undulate leaves	November and December	Pale green panicle, not conspicuous

Arnold-Foster (1948) wrote of *Olearia*: 'No genus has more to offer for windy maritime gardens than this. *Olearia* can provide some of the best of shelter-plants for such climates, and a few of them rank among the most beautiful flowering shrubs we grow.' Arnold-Foster was referring to Cornwall, Devon, the west of Scotland and parts of Ireland.

Brachyglottis Dunedin Group 'Sunshine' and *B. monroi* are frequently grown in ground-cover schemes in amenity sites, particularly in maritime areas.[1]

Berberidaceae Barberry

A family of hardy shrubs used in landscape schemes in western and northern Europe. Two are of importance, *Berberis* and *Mahonia*.

WORLD DISTRIBUTION. North America, South America, Europe, China and Japan.

TYPES OF PLANTS. Shrubs: small, medium or large shrubs.

LEAVES. Foliage is deciduous or evergreen. In *Berberis* some leaves have spine-like margins. *Berberis* also have spines with 1–3–7 prongs located at the axils of leaves. In some species, such as *B. julianae*, they are some 2 cm long. Evergreen, pinnate, holly-like leaves distinguish *Mahonia* from *Berberis*. Autumn colour is a feature of some deciduous species, such as *B. thunbergii*.

FLOWERS. Both genera flower from winter to early summer, producing yellow or orange flowers. Flowers are solitary, in racemes, panicles, corymbs or spikes.

Some are very striking in flower, either the individual flower, e.g. *B. candidula* with round 1 cm across sulphur-yellow flowers, or an orange pendulous cluster of flowers, as in *B. darwinii*.

Depending on the species, flowers in *Mahonia* are erect, ascending or spreading panicles or racemes borne near the apices of lateral or terminal stems. Flowers of *Mahonia* are fragrant. *Mahonia* flower over several months (Table 4.3).

FRUIT. *Mahonia* and *Berberis* bear berries. In *Mahonia* they are held in drooping clusters, the common name Oregon grape is apt. In Norway, *Mahonia aquifolium* was particularly noticeable in fruit, more so than in Britain and Ireland. Depending on the species, berries of *Berberis* are red, translucent amber or blue-bloomed, carried from mid-summer until winter.

---

[1] The species of *Brachyglottis* listed above were previously classified in the genus *Senecio*; some nurseries and garden centres continue to use the latter name.

Table 4.3. Sequence of flower of *Mahonia* from November/December to April/May.

Mahonia lomariifolia: with tall architectural habit and pinnate dark green leaves. Yellow flowers in upright racemes 20–30 cm long
Mahonia 'Charity': foliage not as long as *M. lomariifolia*, with tall upright racemes, yellow flower. A hybrid of *Mahonia japonica* × *M. lomariifolia*, with the habit of the shrub more inclined to the latter.
Mahonia japonica: wide-spreading racemes of yellow flowers.
Mahonia aquifolium: short stumpy racemes of yellow flowers with pinnate leaves and good bushy habit, useful for ground cover

FUNCTIONAL AND ORNAMENTAL USES.
Barrier planting schemes   *Mahonia* 'Charity'
Ground-cover schemes   *B. candidula*

GROWING CONDITIONS. *Mahonia* and *Berberis* are not fastidious about soil conditions.
    Mahonia are useful for shade. Foliage can be damaged by salt spray.

MANAGEMENT. They can be pruned and will regenerate. They tend to fruit best when planted in groups rather than as single plants. They are not cultivated in some countries because of the safety of operatives. Being spined shrubs, *Berberis* can attract litter, plastic bags in particular.

PARTICULAR PLANTING SCHEMES OR PLANT ASSOCIATIONS. In a German town, *B. thunbergii* and *B. thunbergii* f. *atropurpurea* were planted in alternate blocks at a suburban terminus of a tramline.
    The deciduous *B. thunbergii* and evergreen *B. calliantha* and *B. darwinii* are cultivated as hedges.
    B. candidula, with a dense growth habit, and *B. calliantha*, with a more open habit, are seen in ground-cover schemes.
    B. darwinii, *B. thunbergii*, *M.* 'Charity', *M. japonica* and *M. aquifolium* are widely available. Others, such as *B. valdiviana* and *B. hookeri*, are worth seeking out as medium to large shrubs with good flowers and attractive foliage, respectively.

Betulaceae Birch

Deciduous trees, male and female catkins are borne on bare wood in late winter and early spring. In general, they are medium to large and used as street trees and parkland trees and in native and naturalistic schemes (Table 4.4). Trees from the *Betulaceae* are cultivated for functional and ornamental uses.

TYPES OF PLANTS. Medium–large trees, *Alnus*, *Betula*, *Carpinus* and *Corylus*.

Table 4.4. Trees from the *Betulaceae* cultivated for functional and ornamental uses.

Species	Common name	Functional use	Ornamental use	Size (m)
Betula albosinensis var. *septentrionalis*		Parkland tree	Red/plum-stemmed specimen tree	20
Betula ermannii			White-stemmed specimen tree	20
Betula pendula	Weeping birch	Mass planting, reclamation sites	White-stemmed specimen tree	20–30
B. pendula 'Youngii'			Weeping specimen tree	5–8
Betula pubescens	Downy birch	Mass planting, reclamation sites		10–20
Betula utilis	Himalayan birch	Landscape tree	White-stemmed specimen tree	15
B. utilis var. *jacquemontii*	Himalayan birch	Landscape tree	White-stemmed specimen tree	12–15
Alnus cordata	Italian alder	Landscape tree	Glossy green foliage	25
Alnus glutinosa	Alder	Mass planting, reclamation sites		20
Alnus incana	Grey alder	Mass planting, reclamation sites		25
A. incana 'Aurea'			Specimen tree	5–8
A. incana 'Laciniata'			Specimen tree	8–10
Carpinus betulus	Hornbeam	Parkland tree, hedge		25–30
C. betulus 'Fastigiata'		Street tree		20–25
Corylus avellana	Hazel			10–12
C. avellana 'Aurea'			Specimen tree with yellow foliage	5–8
C. avellana 'Contorta'	Contorted hazel		Specimen shrub, a curiosity	2–3
Corylus colurna	Turkish hazel	Street tree		20
Corylus maxima 'Purpurea'			Specimen tree with purple foliage	8–10

WORLD DISTRIBUTION. North temperate regions, some species occur in North America, USA and Canada, others in China and in Europe. *Alnus*, *Corylus* and *Betula* are native in Western Europe.

LEAVES. Deciduous leaves are alternate, simple, entire, some with serrated margins. The leaf veins are generally prominent.

Alnus leaves are often shiny and broad. Winter buds are stalked, a distinguishing feature from the other genera in the family (Fig. 4.3).

Betula leaves are often triangular in outline and thin in texture. Winter buds are small.

Carpinus leaves are oblong-ovate in shape, with 15 pairs of parallel-ribbed leaves. Winter buds are sharp-pointed with overlapping scales.

Corylus leaves are round in outline, often hairy to the touch. Winter buds are ovoid.

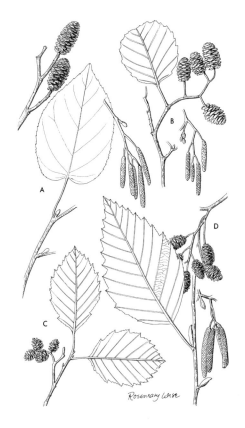

Fig. 4.3. (A) *Alnus cordata*, Italian alder; (B) *Alnus glutinosa*, common alder; (C) *Alnus incana*, grey alder; (D) *Alnus rubra*, red or Oregon alder. (From Savill, 1991.)

FLOWERS. Unisexual flowers are borne in early spring before the leaves emerge. Male flowers are held in erect or pendulous catkins and female flowers in erect catkins.

FRUIT. A small or large nut, sometimes conspicuous, sometimes not, occurs in these trees.

Alnus fruit are green woody 'cones', turning brown as winter progresses and held on the tree for several months and occasionally to the following season.

Betula fruit are very tiny but the overall catkin can be several centimetres long. Seed is shed over the winter months and the catkin disintegrates on the tree.

Corylus fruit is the common hazelnut, with two nuts fused together and enveloped within a leaf-like involucre.

Carpinus fruit are tiny nutlets held in a pendulous catkin, each nutlet enveloped in a green leafy bract.

BARK. The bark is white in several species of *Betula* (birch), making them important trees for winter interest in amenity planting schemes. Shaggy peeling bark occurs in *Betula nigra* (river birch). A thick cork-like bark is a feature of *Corylus colurna* (Turkish hazel).

GROWTH RATE AND LONGEVITY. They are fast-growing and generally short-lived, 40–50 years.

FUNCTIONAL AND ORNAMENTAL USES.

Parkland trees	*Betula pendula* and *B. pendula* 'Dalecarlica', *Carpinus betulus*
Street trees	*C. betulus* 'Fastigiata', *B. pendula* and *Corylus colurna*
Specimen trees for winter interest	*Betula utilis* var. *jacquemontii* and *B. ermanii*
Native/naturalistic planting schemes	*Corylus avellana*, *B. pendula*, *B. pubescens* and *Alnus glutinosa*
Damp sites, soil stabilization and reclamation sites	*Alnus incana* and *B. pendula*
Specimen trees for autumn colour	*B. pendula*

Garden trees	Some particular forms of *Alnus* have been selected: *A. incana* 'Aurea', with yellow leaves and orange-coloured young shoots and catkins, and *A. incana* 'Laciniata', with dainty cut-leaved foliage.
Hedges	*Carpinus betulus*

GROWING CONDITIONS. *Alnus* thrive in moist soils. They can fix atmospheric nitrogen.

B. pendula is an early colonizer of bare ground and requires plenty of light. It grows in poor sandy soils.

B. pubescens and *B. nigra* are suited to damp soils.

MANAGEMENT. See the section in Chapter 5, Trees: Selection, Use and Management.

PESTS AND DISEASES. In *Betula*, distorted growth forming a witches' broom is caused by *Phytoptus rudis*, an insect.

PARTICULAR PLANTING SCHEMES OR PLANT ASSOCIATIONS. At Mount Usher, Couny Wicklow, Ireland, a specimen tree *Betula maximowicziana* of some 20 m tall is well positioned by a pond with a backdrop of taller trees.

Native woodland of *B. pendula* occurs in many parts of Ireland and Scotland.

Corylus avellana (hazel) clothes some of the extensive limestone pavement of the Burren, County Clare, Ireland.

Extensive hedges of *Carpinus betulus* (hornbeam), known as *charmilles*, form part of the baroque gardens in Versailles and Vaux-le-Vicomte, France, Sans Souci, Potsdam, Germany, and Belvedere and Schönbrunn, Vienna, Austria.

——————————— • ———————————

Buddlejaceae Buddleja[1]

A monotypic genus of flowering shrubs, some are suited to general landscape schemes and others are only suitable for sites with good growing conditions.

TYPES OF PLANTS. Shrubs: medium to large.

WORLD DISTRIBUTION. China, Himalaya and South Africa.

LEAVES. Foliage is evergreen and opposite, except in *Buddleja alternifolia*, where it is alternate.

---

[1] Formerly *Buddleia* and still so in some nursery catalogues.

Table 4.5. Main species of *Buddleja* suitable for cultivation use in landscape schemes.

Genus	Foliage	Flower	Time of flower	Size (m)	Country of origin
Buddleja alternifolia	Deciduous, alternate in arching branches	Lilac flowers studded on arching stems of previous year's growth	June	3–6	China
Buddleja auriculata	Evergreen	Pale butterscotch-yellow flowers	Winter	2–4	South Africa
Buddleja colvilei	Deciduous	Terminal panicles of deep red flowers	June	2	Himalaya
Buddleja davidii	Deciduous, large lanceolate leaves	Panicles of mauve flowers	July–Sept.	2–3	China
Buddleja globosa	Deciduous	Balls of orange flowers	May	3	Chile

FLOWERS. These are held in tubular panicles or ball-like clusters.

FRUIT. A narrow capsule, not of ornamental interest.

GROWTH RATE AND LONGEVITY. They are fast-growing to very fast-growing and vigorous.

FUNCTIONAL AND ORNAMENTAL USES. (Table 4.5)
General landscape shrub   *Buddleja globosa*
Wildlife gardens   *B. davidii*
Select shrub for sheltered sites *B. colvilei*

GROWING CONDITIONS. *B. davidii* grows in very poor soil conditions, particularly in derelict urban areas. A position close to a sheltered wall is required for tender species such as *B. colvilei*.

MANAGEMENT. As *B. davidii* flowers on young wood, it should be coppiced to ground level in March. Others are pruned when they become too large for their allotted area.

PARTICULAR PLANTING SCHEMES OR PLANT ASSOCIATIONS. *B. davidii* is self-sown in cities and towns in drainpipes, crevices in walls, waste grounds and neglected open space. Due to its attraction to butterflies, it is commonly called the butterfly bush.

Buxaceae Box

They are evergreen shrubs useful as a foil for other shrubs and in particular for shaded situations where little else will thrive.

TYPES OF PLANTS. Shrub: small to medium to rarely large-sized.

WORLD DISTRIBUTION. Europe, North Africa, Western Asia, Japan and China.

LEAVES. Foliage is evergreen, opposite or alternate, lanceolate shiny in *Sarcococca*, toothed in *Pachysandra* and entire in *Buxus*. Foliage of *Buxus* has a musty smell. Hard, mid-green leaves on stiff stems distinguish *Buxus* from *Lonicera nitida* (*Caprifoliaceae*), often erroneously called box, which has tiny dark green leaves on thin pliable stems.

FLOWERS. Greenish-coloured, small flowers occur in *Buxus* and *Pachysandra*. In *Sarcococca*, the flowers are scented, white with small strap-like petals.

FRUIT. *Buxus* and *Pachysandra* bear green fruit. *Sarcococca* flowers and fruits at the same time during the winter months. *Sarcococca* has fleshy red/black fruit. The styles persist on the fruit, in appearance like tiny curved horns.

GROWTH RATE AND LONGEVITY. They are generally slow-growing. *Buxus* is long-lived and large tree-like specimens dating from the 19th century occur in public parks and in private estates.

FUNCTIONAL AND ORNAMENTAL USES.

Topiary	*Buxus sempervirens*
Formal hedges	*B. sempervirens* 'Suffruticosa'
Winter flowering and fruiting shrub	*Sarcococca*
Variegated shrubs	*B. sempervirens* 'Aureovariegata'
Ground cover	*Sarcococca confusa* and *Pachysandra terminalis*

GROWING CONDITIONS. They grow best in fertile soil. *Pachysandra* grows well in semi-shaded situations beneath other shrubs, where it forms a pretty green ground-cover. Where it is 'happy' it grows well, and where it is a poor 'doer' it is best to replant with another shrub.

Buxus grows in shaded and in open situations.

MANAGEMENT. Hedges have to be trimmed carefully. Avoid petrol-driven hedge cutters as the petrol fumes can damage the hedge.

Where a hedge has not been trimmed for many years it is advisable to cut one side, then the other and finally the top portion.

PARTICULAR PLANTING SCHEMES OR PLANT ASSOCIATIONS. The formal patterns in the restored Privy Garden, Hampton Court, London and Het Loo, Apeldoorn, the Netherlands, 17th century gardens of King William and Queen Mary, are etched in *B. sempervirens*.

Many fine examples of *B. sempervirens* globes, pillars and balls growing in planters and containers occur in inner-city minimalist gardens.

Box hedges at Birr Castle, County Offaly, Ireland, are reputed to be the tallest in the world.

P. terminalis is used extensively in the Netherlands as a ground cover.

—————————————— • ——————————————

Caprifoliaceae Elderberry

In terms of landscape plants this family provides several tough, reliable, widely used shrubs from the following genera: *Abelia* (q.v.); *Lonicera* (honeysuckle) (q.v.); *Sambucus* (elderberry) (q.v.); *Symphoricarpos* (snowberry) (q.v.); *Viburnum* (q.v.) and *Weigela* (q.v.) (Table 4.6).

TYPES OF PLANTS. Trees: shrubby trees 5–7 m tall.
   Shrubs: deciduous and evergreen.
   Climbers: deciduous and evergreen.

WORLD DISTRIBUTION. Cosmopolitan, most genera are native to eastern Asia, eastern North America and Western Europe. Some species are native to Britain and Ireland.

LEAVES. Foliage is opposite without stipules. An exception is *Sambucus* with pinnate leaves and stipules.

FLOWERS. These are held in a panicle, with a tubular corolla of four to five lobes. Lobes are short in *Sambucus* and sometimes have a very pronounced tube, as in *Lonicera* (honeysuckle). Many are sweetly scented. Depending on the genus and on the species within genera, they flower throughout the year.

FRUIT. Some have a fleshy berry or drupe, as in *Sambucus* (elderberry) and *Viburnum*. In others, e.g. *Weigela*, the fruit is dry.

Table 4.6. Genera from the *Caprifoliaceae* commonly cultivated in landscape schemes.

Genus	Tree	Shrub	Climber	Leaves	D	E	Flower colour	Scent	Time of flowering	Type of fruit
Abelia		x		Entire,		x	Pink		Autumn	
Lonicera		x	x	Entire thin texture	x	x	Yellow, orange, deep pink	Fragrance in some	Summer	Red-indigo berries
Sambucus	x	x		Pinnate	x		White	Musty	Spring	Black, autumn
Symphoricarpos		x				x	Tiny pink/ white		Early summer	White/pink autumn
Viburnum		x		Glabrous or hairy	x	x	White/pink	Fragrance in some	Winter to autumn	Red, blue, black translucent
Weigela		x				x	Pink, white, red		Early summer	Dry capsular

D, deciduous foliage; E, evergreen foliage.

GROWTH RATE AND LONGEVITY. They are fast-growing and live for many years.

FUNCTIONAL AND ORNAMENTAL USES.

Ground-cover schemes	*Viburnum davidii*
Medium-sized shrubs in shrubberies	*Weigela florida*
Hedging plants	*V. tinus*
Native material and naturalistic schemes	*V. opulus. Symphoricarpos albus* (snowberry) has become naturalized in parts of Ireland

GROWING CONDITIONS. They will grow in variable soil conditions. They will withstand exposure to wind, but not salt spray.

MANAGEMENT. Pruning requirements are few. When necessary they can be pruned severely and will regenerate.

PESTS AND DISEASES. These are few. Sudden oak death *Phytophthora ramorum* occurs on some species of *Viburnum*.

OTHER GENERA. *Leycesteria formosa*, though not native, has become naturalized in some places. It is a useful shrub for rough areas but it can become invasive.

Abelia

TYPES OF PLANTS. Shrubs.

WORLD DISTRIBUTION. China, Himalaya, Mexico.

LEAVES. Opposite foliage is evergreen or semi-evergreen, ovate in shape and sometimes rather shiny.

FLOWERS. Solitary or clusters of flowers are borne in leaf axils. Sepals (two to five) are conspicuous, lasting after the funnel or campanulate flower has faded. Flowers are pink and the sepals are reddish-coloured.

FRUIT. Not noticeable.

GROWTH RATE AND LONGEVITY. Medium growth rate.

FUNCTIONAL AND ORNAMENTAL USES.
Depending on the species, they are early summer to autumn flowering shrubs. They are long-lasting in flower.

GROWING CONDITIONS. They grow best in a sheltered situation.

MANAGEMENT. Little pruning is required, except for the occasional removal of straggly stems.

PARTICULAR PLANTING SCHEMES OR PLANT ASSOCIATIONS. In recent years this has become a frequently planted shrub for autumn interest. Common taxa available in the trade are *Abelia* × *grandiflora*, *A.* × *grandiflora* 'Francis Mason' and *A.* × *grandiflora* 'Gold Spot'.

Lonicera (honeysuckle)

TYPES OF PLANTS. Shrubs: small to medium-sized.
   Climbers.

WORLD DISTRIBUTION. China, Japan, Europe and western North America.

LEAVES. Small to medium in size and thin in texture, they are usually elliptic to lanceolate in shape, often with conspicuous venation.

FLOWERS. They are arranged in pairs or whorls of tubular or campanulate, yellow, orange or deep pink flowers. They are summer-flowering and some are sweetly scented.

FRUIT. Fruit, which is held in pairs or in small clusters, is a juicy berry, red or indigo in colour.

GROWTH RATE AND LONGEVITY. They are fast-growing and live for many years.

FUNCTIONAL AND ORNAMENTAL USES.

Hedges	*Lonicera nitida*
Ground-cover	*L. pileata*
Climbing plants	*L. japonica* 'Aureoreticulata', *L. henryi* and *L. sempervirens*
Native planting schemes	*L. periclymenum* (woodbine, columbine or honeysuckle) of hedgerows in rural areas
Winter-flowering shrub	*L. standishii*

GROWING CONDITIONS. Shrubby species are easy to establish and grow well in most situations, except where salt-laden winds prevail. Some climbing species can be slow to flower.

MANAGEMENT. On climbing species remove straggly growth each year. The evergreen shrubby species can be severally pruned and will regenerate.

PARTICULAR PLANTING SCHEMES OR PLANT ASSOCIATIONS. *L. nitida* is a common hedging plant in older parts of Dublin city.
   L. pileata is widely used as a ground cover or pruned into a flat low hedge. It is a modern-day equivalent of a Victorian laurel lawn, where *Prunus laurocerasus* was trimmed to a height of about a metre.

Lonicera involucrata (with conspicuous ornamental bracts) and *L. henryi* are commonly grown as a landscape shrub and evergreen climber in Norway.

Sambucus (elderberry)

TYPES OF PLANTS. Shrubby trees.

WORLD DISTRIBUTION. Western Asia and Europe.

LEAVES. Leaves are opposite, pinnate with five to seven leaflets. Foliage of *Sambucus nigra* (elderberry) has a rancid smell.

FLOWERS. A white cyme distinguishes *S. nigra* (elderberry) from *S. racemosa* (red-berried elder), which has a conical inflorescence.

FRUIT. Black (*S. nigra*) or red fruits (*S. racemosa*) are borne in autumn.

BARK. Rugged bark is rough to the touch. The interior of young shoots is hollow.

GROWTH RATE AND LONGEVITY. They are fast-growing. *S. nigra* (elderberry) can become invasive and can be very difficult to eradicate.

FUNCTIONAL AND ORNAMENTAL USES. Native or naturalistic schemes: *S. nigra* (elderberry) and *S. racemosa* (red-berried elder).
Several cultivars with attractive delicately cut leaves have been selected, e.g. *S. nigra* f. *laciniata* and *S. racemosa* 'Plumosa Aurea'.
Purple foliage: *S. nigra* 'Guincho Purple' is a fast-growing cultivar with flowers tinged pink and foliage holding its colour until leaf fall.

GROWING CONDITIONS. They grow in a wide range of situations.

MANAGEMENT. To maintain as a shrub, stems can be coppiced annually. It is very vigorous and will 'elbow out' its neighbours.

Symphoricarpos

TYPES OF PLANTS. Shrubs.

WORLD DISTRIBUTION. North America.

LEAVES. Foliage is deciduous, opposite, thinly textured. Leaf venation is prominent, as in *Lonicera*.

FLOWERS. Pink or white, insignificant, tubular flowers are borne in early summer.

FRUIT. White or pink hollow dry berries are conspicuous in autumn and winter.

GROWTH RATE AND LONGEVITY. Fast-growing and long-lived.

FUNCTIONAL AND ORNAMENTAL USES.

Ground cover	*Symphoricarpos* × *chenaultii* 'Hancock' is an excellent, rapidly growing, impenetrable and dense ground cover, in both summer and winter.
Landscape shrubs for industrial sites	They are too vigorous for small spaces or garden schemes.
Variegated shrub	*S. orbiculatus* 'Foliis Variegatis': colour of variegation is held until leaf fall. Dense twiggy growth of brown stems is noticeable in winter.

GROWING CONDITIONS. They grow well in shade and in poor soils.

MANAGEMENT. The shrubs can be severely pruned and will regenerate rapidly.

PARTICULAR PLANTING SCHEMES OR PLANT ASSOCIATIONS. *Symphoricarpos* × *chenaultii* 'Hancock' is used as ground cover in hotel grounds, lining pathways and separating cars and pedestrians (Braunschweig, Germany). It is also used in The Netherlands.

S. albus (snowberry), a weedy plant common in old gardens and estates. It is a difficult plant to eradicate, though the white berries can be attractive in winter.

Viburnum

TYPES OF PLANTS. Shrubs.

Viburnum is an important genus of 150 species of deciduous and evergreen shrubs, with a variety of shrubs suitable for a variety of situations. By careful selection of species and cultivars, a succession of flowering can be achieved from winter to late summer (Table 4.7).

WORLD DISTRIBUTION. Eastern North America, Japan, China and Europe.

LEAVES. They are deciduous or evergreen, some have prominent veins, some are partly hairy while others are densely felted.

FLOWERS. The many flowered inflorescence is axillary or terminal. Some *Viburnum* have enlarged sterile flowers at the margin of the flower head. The corolla is tubular and flower colour is white, greenish white or pale to deep pink. Some are fragrant.

FRUIT. Two forms of fruit occur, dry fruit or a juicy drupe, coloured blue, black or translucent.

Table 4.7. Yearly sequence of flower and fruit in the genus *Viburnum*.

Name	Foliage	Time of year	Flower colour	Fruit	Time of year
Viburnum farreri	Evergreen	November–January	Pink, scented		
Viburnum tinus	Evergreen	November–January	White		
V. tinus 'Variegatum'	Evergreen	January	White		
Viburnum × *burkwoodii*	Evergreen	January–April	Pink-budded white flowers, scented		
Viburnum carlesii	Evergreen	March–May	Pink-budded white flowers, scented		
Viburnum davidii	Evergreen, distinct venation	May–June	White	Blue	Late summer
Viburnum cinnamomifolium	Evergreen	May–June	White		
Viburnum rhytidophyllum	Evergreen, large felted leaves	May	Dull white	Red, then black	Late summer
Viburnum lantana	Deciduous	May–June	Dull white		
Viburnum betulifolium	Deciduous	June	White	Translucent orange	Late summer–winter
Viburnum opulus	Deciduous, maple-like foliage	June–July	White	Red	Late summer–winter
Viburnum plicatum	Deciduous, autumn colour	May–June	White in the shape of a tennis ball		
V. plicatum f. *tomentosum*	Deciduous	May–June	White, broad, flat flower head		
V. plicatum f. *tomentosum* 'Mariesii'	Deciduous	May–June	As above		
Viburnum erubescens	Evergreen	July	White	Translucent amber	Late summer

GROWTH RATE AND LONGEVITY. They are fast-growing. Shrubs 40–50 years old occur in plant collections.

FUNCTIONAL AND ORNAMENTAL USES.

Small- to medium- to large-sized evergreen shrubs	*Viburnum carlesii, V. tinus* and *V. rhytidophyllum,* respectively
Ground-cover shrubs	*V. davidii*
Native and naturalistic schemes	*V. opulus* and *V. lantana*

Damp sites	*V. opulus* (guelder rose or water elder)
Autumn colour	*V. plicatum*
Architectural, horizontal spreading habit	*V. plicatum* and its cultivars
Fruiting shrub	*V. betulifolium*

GROWING CONDITIONS. They grow in a wide variety of situations.

MANAGEMENT. To ensure good fruiting, plant in large numbers to ensure cross-pollination. Some forms of particular species are better than others, e.g. some *V. davidii* are shy-flowering.

Where they outgrow their allotted space, they can be pruned moderately to severely and will regrow.

PESTS AND DISEASES. Sudden oak death *Phytophthora ramorum* occurs on some *Viburnum*.

PARTICULAR PLANTING SCHEMES OR PLANT ASSOCIATIONS. At Fernhill Gardens, Dublin, tree-sized, rosy pink-flowered *Rhododendron arboreum* are a foil for a row of well-spaced *V. plicatum*; as the *Rhododendron* flowers fade, the *Viburnum* break into leaf and then into flower.

Weigela

TYPES OF PLANTS. Medium-sized shrubs with an upright habit.

WORLD DISTRIBUTION. Eastern Asia.

LEAVES. Foliage is deciduous, green, variegated or purple in colour.

FLOWERS. They are borne in early summer. They are tubular at the base and campanulate at the mouth, in shades of red, pink or white.

FRUIT. Fruit is a narrow capsule, not of ornamental value.

GROWTH RATE AND LONGEVITY. They are fast-growing. They can be grown for 15–20 years before becoming woody and over-mature in appearance.

FUNCTIONAL AND ORNAMENTAL USES. Early summer-flowering shrubs for general landscape situations.

GROWING CONDITIONS. They are easy to cultivate.

MANAGEMENT. They require little pruning. Where cultivars are cultivated, shoots that have reverted to the species should be removed.

PARTICULAR PLANTING SCHEMES OR PLANT ASSOCIATIONS. Now less frequently planted, it occurs in established schemes along with shrubby species of other genera.

Common taxa available in the trade include *Weigela* 'Florida Variegata', *Weigela* 'Bristol Ruby' and *Weigela florida* 'Foliis Purpureis'.

–––––––––––––––––––––– • ––––––––––––––––––––––

Celastraceae Spindle Bush

One genus *Euonymus,* is commonly grown in urban areas as an evergreen ground-cover and/or as a deciduous shrubby tree in rural areas. The angled pink seed with orange seed within is distinctive.

TYPES OF PLANTS. Trees: small.
     Shrubs: small to medium.

WORLD DISTRIBUTION. China, Japan and Europe.

LEAVES. Foliage is deciduous and evergreen. Foliage is opposite and in the evergreen species glossy and stiff to the touch. *Euonymus europaeus* and *E. alatus* develop striking shades of deep pink in autumn.

FLOWERS. The overall inflorescence is showy, in shades of yellow or whitish yellow. The parts of the individual flowers are in units of four or five.

FRUIT. Reddish or deep pink seed capsules are three- or five-lobed. The lobes are often angled and an individual capsule is similar to a three-cornered hat. The seed capsule splits to reveal an orange seed (aril) within, an unusual colour combination.

BARK. Ribs of cork running on the margins of the stem are attractive in winter. *E. alatus* is a particular example.

GROWTH RATE AND LONGEVITY. Medium growth rate and they are long-lived.

FUNCTIONAL AND ORNAMENTAL USES.

Native shrubs	*E. europaeus*
Hedge	*E. japonicus, E. fortunei*
Ground-cover	*E. fortunei* and some cultivars, e.g. *E. fortunei* 'Emerald Gaiety' and *E. fortunei* 'Emerald and Gold'
Autumn colour	*E. europaeus* and *E. alatus*
Tiny-leaved shrubs	*E. japonicus* 'Microphyllus'

GROWING CONDITIONS. They grow in poor situations.

MANAGEMENT. They require little pruning unless they outgrow their allotted area.

PARTICULAR PLANTING SCHEMES OR PLANT ASSOCIATIONS. It is a widely used ground-cover on the campus of University College Dublin, where it lines many pathways and roads. The ability of *E. fortunei* cultivars to revert to the species and develop 'sports' is clearly visible in these schemes.

E. japonicus is often seen as a free-standing shrub or a hedge in older suburban gardens and parks in Dublin and other cities.

E. fortunei var. *vegetus* has thick, glossy, green leaves, a puzzle at first sight, especially as some shoots are spreading and others are upright. It is grown as a ground-cover in the Netherlands.

--- • ---

Cistaceae Rock Rose

The genus *Cistus* provides small- to medium-sized shrubs suitable for dry conditions. *Helianthemum* is a vigorous flat-growing ground-cover.

TYPES OF PLANTS. Shrubs: small- to medium-sized shrubs.

WORLD DISTRIBUTION. Mediterranean region.

LEAVES. Foliage is evergreen and opposite. Leaves exude a sticky resin, which is often scented and more apparent on hot dry days.

FLOWERS. Flowers are arranged in cymes and each one has three to five sepals and five petals. Depending on the species or cultivar, flowers are in shades of pink, yellow or white, often with a yellow or red blotch at the base of the petals. Flowers are borne in early summer.

FRUIT. Fruit is a capsule, not striking from an ornamental point of view.

GROWTH RATE AND LONGEVITY. Medium growth rate and short-lived.

FUNCTIONAL AND ORNAMENTAL USES.

Fast-growing ground-cover sub-shrubs	*Helianthemum*
Ground-cover shrub	*Cistus*
Summer-flowering shrubs	*Cistus* and *Helianthemum*

GROWING CONDITIONS. They grow best in hot dry conditions and in free-draining soils. *Cistus* require little or no pruning, but can be pruned after flowering. If *Helianthemum* outgrows its allotted space, it can be given a 'short back and sides' with a hedge trimmer or Strimmer™ and will quickly regrow.

PARTICULAR PLANTING SCHEMES OR PLANT ASSOCIATIONS. *Helianthemum nummularium* is native in Britain.

Many hybrids have been raised, of which *H.* 'Rhodanthe Carneum' and *H.* 'Wisley Primrose' are two examples.

Some of the more common *Cistus* include *C.* × *argenteus* 'Silver Pink', *C.* × *pulverulentus* 'Sunset' and *C. ladanifer*.

———————————— • ————————————

Cornaceae Dogwoods

Some shrubs from this family are tough and hardy and suitable for general use in landscape schemes. Others are worth growing as summer-flowering shrubs but careful site selection is crucial.

TYPES OF PLANTS. Shrubs: medium to very large shrubs.
Trees: 5–8 m.

WORLD DISTRIBUTION. China, Japan, USA and Europe (*Cornus*), New Zealand (*Griselinia* and *Corokia*), Japan (*Aucuba*).

LEAVES. Opposite, sometimes alternate, some are deciduous, others evergreen. Veined leaves are a characteristic of *Cornus*. *Griselinia* has lime-green leaves, smooth to the touch. *Corokia* has a greyish cast to the foliage and has a whitish hairy undersurface to the leaf (Table 4.8).

FLOWERS. Flowers are small and occur on axillary or terminal panicles. Showy bracts are a feature of many of the tender *Cornus*. *Griselinia* has greenish, insignificant flowers. *Corokia* has deep yellow, tiny, star-shaped flowers.

FRUIT. Fruit is a drupe or berry. Fruits are conspicuous in *Cornus alba*, with a cluster of white fruits at the tips of shoots, and in *Cornus mas* (cornelian cherry), with red fruits, shaped like a cherry, but ovoid rather than round. *Aucuba* also has red cherry-like fruit. The fruit of *Corokia* is small and orange in colour.

Table 4.8. Key characteristics of genera from the *Cornaceae*.

Genus	Foliage	Flower	Fruit	Function
Aucuba	Evergreen, opposite	Male reddish-brown petals	Red berry	Shrubbery in shade
Cornus	Deciduous and evergreen, alternate and opposite	Mass of yellow stamens, sometimes with conspicuous white bracts	Drupe, white in *Cornus alba*, red in *Cornus mas* and *Cornus controversa*	Some for mass planting, some for select situations
Corokia	Evergreen, alternate	Yellow, star-like	Orange	Shrubbery in maritime area
Griselinia	Evergreen, alternate	Green, insignificant	Berry (only occurs in the mildest areas)	Very large shrub, hedge

GROWTH RATE AND LONGEVITY. *Aucuba japonica, Cornus alba* and *Griselinia littoralis* are fast growing and long lived.

FUNCTIONAL AND ORNAMENTAL USES.

Landscape shrubs for difficult situations	*C. alba, C. stolonifera* and *A. japonica*
Shrubs for maritime areas	*G. littoralis*
Damp sites	*C. alba* and *C. sericea*
Hedging	*Griselinia*
Variegated shrubs	*A. japonica* 'Variegata', *Cornus controversa* 'Variegata', *Cornus alternifolia* 'Variegata'
Summer-flowering shrubs	*Cornus kousa*
Specimen tree for sheltered site	*C. controversa*
Special plants for special places	*C. controversa, Cornus* 'Porlock' and *C. kousa*
Autumn colour	*Cornus florida*

GROWING CONDITIONS. Damp sites for *C. alba*, others require milder conditions and garden situations. *Corokia* and *Griselinia* grow well in maritime areas but in inland areas could be damaged by frosts.

MANAGEMENT. Where *Cornus alba* (dogwood) is cultivated for its red shoots, an annual coppicing of stems is necessary each spring.

PARTICULAR PLANTING SCHEMES OR PLANT ASSOCIATIONS. *C. alba* is frequently planted on motorways in Ireland. In some situations it is used to signal an interchange to motorists.

Huge examples of *Griselinia littoralis* some 8–10 m tall occur in gardens in the south-west of Ireland. *Griselinia* is a common hedging plant in parts of Dublin. Too often, however, space is limited and it has become the 'wrong hedge in the wrong place'.

A. japonica 'Variegata' is seen in basement gardens in London, where plants are prone to periods of high temperatures and little precipitation.

Corokia has become more common in recent years. They are evergreen shrubs with star-like yellow flowers and orange fruit. *Corokia cotoneaster* is slow-growing and suitable where spaced is very limited. *C.* × *virgata* is an upright shrub with dense branches and a greyish cast to its small spoon-shaped foliage.

Cupressaceae Cypress

They are densely branched evergreen trees, with tiny scale-like foliage, often with distinctive tree shapes (Fig. 2.15).

TYPES OF PLANTS. Trees: small to very large trees.
  Shrubs: many cultivars selected as dwarf conifers.

WORLD DISTRIBUTION. Western North America, Europe, China and Japan.

LEAVES. Foliage is evergreen, scale-leaved with one tiny scale slotting into the next. The scale leaves combine to create frond-like branches, which clothe the tree. *Chamaecyparis* are distinguished by a translucent gland, which is situated where two leaves meet. This translucent gland is visible when one places a leaf between one's fingers and looks through the leaf towards the sky or a bright light. In *Juniperus* (juniper) young foliage is awl-shaped and scale-like on older shoots. In *Juniperus communis* (common juniper), the foliage always remains awl-shaped. Foliage colour is green, with glaucous, yellow and variegated forms occuring among the cultivars of *Chamaecyparis* and *Thuja* species (Table 4.9).

FLOWERS. Male strobili are composed of tiny pollen sacs; on closer inspection they look like yellow droplets and they are borne at the tips of shoots. In one Lawson cypress cultivar, *Chamaecyparis lawsoniana* 'Wisselii', the tree takes on a reddish sheen as pollen is shed in early spring. A similar effect develops later in spring with *Cupressus arizonica* var. *glabra*, which has a yellowish sheen: an ephemeral ornamental feature, but noticeable none the less.

FRUIT. Cones are globose or ellipsoid, with six to 12 shield-like scales fitting closely together. Depending on the genus, each scale is marked with either a flat ridge or a conspicuous hook. The genus *Juniperus* bears purple berries.

BARK. Given the usually densely branched nature of the trees, bark is not readily visible. In old specimens of *Cupressus macrocarpa*, bark is grey. In *C. arizonica* var. *glabra*, bark is an attractive plum colour, noticeable even on youngish trees.

GROWTH RATE AND LONGEVITY. Members of this family have a medium growth rate and are long-lived.

Table 4.9. Foliage and fruit in genera of the *Cupressaceae*.

Genus	Foliage	Fruit
Chamaecyparis	Flattened sprays	Globular with a curved spine
× *Cupressocyparis*	Partly flattened and held around the stem	Rarely seen
Cupressus	Foliage held around the shoot	Round, woody, 6–12 shield-like scales, remaining on the tree for many years
Juniperus	Often acicular or scale-like	Berry
Thuja	Foliage flattened and with a white X on the undersurface of the scale-like leaves.	Valvate, each valve opening at the tip of the cone and remaining closed at the base.

FUNCTIONAL AND ORNAMENTAL USES.

Specimen trees	*Cupressus arizonica* var. *glabra, C. macrocapra*
Screening and hedges	× *Cupressocyparis leylandii* (space permitting), *Chamaecyparis lawsoniana* 'Triomf van Boskoop'
Ground cover	*Juniperus communis* and *J.* × *pfitzeriana*
Barrier planting	Especially in the Netherlands and Belgium, where fastigiate forms of *Thuja* and *Chamaecyparis* are used to screen one property from another
Ground cover	The practice of planting dwarf conifers and *Erica* (heather) together in ground-cover schemes is no longer as common as it was in the 1970s and 1980s. Where many of the *Erica* have died out of these schemes, dwarf conifers remain, and one realizes that the term dwarf conifer is a misnomer
Native and naturalistic planting schemes	*Juniperus communis*

GROWING CONDITIONS. Good soil conditions are required and they will withstand atmospheric pollution to a certain degree.

Where one tree has grown into another, or where shrubs have prevented light from reaching the branches, a conifer will lose its leaves and they are very unlikely to regrow.

Juniperus communis grows in extreme conditions. It is native in Ireland, where it occurs on limestone pavement in the Burren, County Clare, as a flat, prostrate shrub. In Northumberland, in the north-east of England, it is a bushy shrub and in Norway and Sweden it is a tall, fastigiate, pencil-shaped tree.

MANAGEMENT. They need regular pruning. Conifers from this family do not regenerate from wood that is more than 3 years old.

PARTICULAR PLANTING SCHEMES OR PLANT ASSOCIATIONS. × *Cupressocyparis leylandii* is grown in the Spanish Garden at Mount Stewart, County Down, Northern Ireland, where it forms a 'live' arched trellis. It is a much maligned tree, too often planted in the wrong place in suburban gardens or as hedges or barrier planting in rural areas. Where it is well maintained as a hedge or has sufficient space to develop as a specimen tree, it is very fine.

Cupressus sempervirens is a hallmark of Italian and southern French landscapes. It is used to some extent as a street tree in southern Europe (Saebø *et al.*, 2005). In recent years it has been grown in landscape schemes in Britain and Ireland.

Members of this family contribute to the range of trees cultivated in Southern and Western Europe (Table 4.10).

Table 4.10. *Cupressaceae* in streets, parks and urban woodland in Europe (from Saebø *et al.* 2005).

Southern Europe	Central Europe	Northern Europe
× *Cupressocyparis leylandii*	× *Cupressocyparis leylandii*	None
Cupressus arizonica (*Cupressus glauca*)	*Juniperus virginiana*	
Cupressus sempervirens	*Chamaecyparis lawsoniana*	
Juniperus oxycedrus		

Ericaceae Heather

A large family of many genera, of which *Rhododendron* and *Pieris* are cultivated in landscape schemes where acidic soil conditions prevail.

TYPES OF PLANTS. Trees, generally shrubs and subshrubs.

WORLD DISTRIBUTION. Himalaya, China, Japan, eastern North America and Europe. Some *Erica* are native to Britain and Ireland and one tree species, *Arbutus unedo*, is native in Ireland.

LEAVES. Evergreen or deciduous.

FLOWERS. Flowers are white and pitcher-shaped in *Arbutus* and *Pieris*. In common landscape rhododendrons, flowers are in terminal clusters, generally funnel-shaped. Flower shape in *Erica*, *Calluna* and *Daboecia* is cylindrical to spherical.

FRUIT. Dry woody capsule in *Rhododendron* and *Pieris*.

FUNCTIONAL AND ORNAMENTAL USES.

Evergreen shrubs in landscape situations where acidic soil occurs	Hardy hybrid rhododendrons
Ground cover	*Erica* (heather), *Calluna* (ling) and *Daboecia* (St Daboec's heath)
Naturalistic planting schemes	*Erica*, *Calluna* and *Daboecia*

GROWING CONDITIONS. They require acidic soil conditions, though some hardy hybrid rhododendrons will tolerate some lime in the soil. *Erica carnea*, a spring-flowering heather, grows in both acidic and alkaline soil.

MANAGEMENT. Prune when shrubs have outgrown their allotted space. Hardy hybrid rhododendrons can be pruned severely and, though they may lose their flowers for a year or two, they will regrow with a flourish. Heathers are given an annual pruning to remove straggly growth.

PARTICULAR PLANTING SCHEMES OR PLANT ASSOCIATIONS. In Madrid *Arbutus andrachne* (madroño) with very red stems is cultivated as a street tree in many city centre streets. They are also growing successfully on Royal Hospital Road, London, an indication of the higher temperatures in an inner-city street.

Arbutus unedo (strawberry tree) occurs in the wild in Killarney National Park, County Kerry, Ireland. A venerable old specimen, estimated to be 400 years old, grows in Killruddery, County Wicklow, Ireland, a 17th century garden. A dome-shaped tree, with evergreen, small, lanceolate leaves, white, pitcher-shaped flowers and a strawberry-like fruit, identifies an *Arbutus*.

Shrubs from the genus *Pieris* form medium to large evergreen shrubs. All have pendulous racemes or panicles of white, pitcher-shaped flowers. As the flowers fade, new foliage of a rich red colour emerges, a striking sight. *Pieris japonica*, with small leaves, is the smallest-growing of the *Pieris* and many cultivars have been selected. They are suitable for the front of a shrubbery. Larger-growing cultivars for the middle to rear of a shrubbery are *Pieris* 'Forest Flame' and *P. formosa* 'Wakehurst'.

Rhododendron ponticum has become naturalized in parts of the west of Ireland, the west of Scotland and parts of Wales. While it forms a tough, hardy hedge, the risks of establishment in the wild associated with *Rhododendron* would question any use of this shrub in landscape schemes, particularly in rural areas. Some 300 species and several hundred more hybrid rhododendrons are in cultivation in specialist collections in Britain and Ireland. Some hybrids in particular, namely the hardy hybrids, e.g. *Rhododendron* 'Cunningham's White', *R.* 'Pink Pearl', *R.* 'Cynthia' and *R.* 'Sappho', and hybrids from *R. yakushimanum*, e.g. *R.* 'Sleepy', *R.* Dopey', *R.* 'Bashful' and *R.* 'Sneezy', are suitable for use in landscape schemes.

Fabaceae Broom, Laburnum and Gorse

A butterfly-shaped flower or pea pod-like seed capsule (legume) denotes a member of this family (Fig. 4.4). The food crops *Pisum sativum* (pea) and *Vicia faba* (broad bean), the forage crops *Vicia* (clover) and *Medicago* (lucerne), the native plants *Lotus corniculatus* (bird's foot trefoil) and *Anthyllis vulneraria* (kidney vetch) and the herbaceous plants *Lathyrus* (sweet pea) and *Lupinus* (lupin) are among the non-woody members of the family.

TYPES OF PLANTS. Trees: 5–20 m.
Shrubs: 50 cm–4 m.
Climbers: Several metres in length.

WORLD DISTRIBUTION. Britain and Ireland, Southern Europe, eastern USA, New Zealand, China.

LEAVES. Foliage is green, alternate and generally pinnate. In some plants, it is highly adapted and becomes small and linear, as in *Cytisus* (some), *Genista* and *Ulex*.

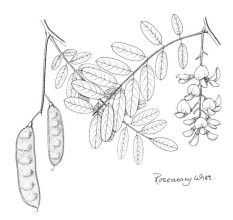

Fig. 4.4. *Robinia pseudoacacia*, false acacia. (From Savill, 1991.)

FLOWERS. A butterfly-shaped flower is a characteristic of the *Papilionoideae* and *Caesalpinioideae* sections of the family, sections most usually grown in landscape situations. The inflorescence is in axillary racemes, e.g. *Cytisus* and *Genista*, or pendulous racemes, e.g. *Laburnum*, *Robinia* and *Wisteria*. Flower colour is usually yellow, pink or mauve, often butterfly-shaped. A mass of stamens, as in *Acacia* (florist's mimosa), is characteristic of the *Mimosoideae* section of the family. *Acacia* is confined to plant collections in southern Britain and Ireland.

FRUIT. In all genera the fruit is a legume (a pea pod is an example). In some genera, such as *Robinia*, the pod is glabrous and several centimetres long; in others, such as *Ulex*, it is short and hairy.

GROWTH RATE AND LONGEVITY. In general, the shrubby genera are fast-growing but short-lived. The tree genera live for 50 or more years, with *Robinia* living for 100 or more years.

FUNCTIONAL AND ORNAMENTAL USES.

Park and amenity trees	*Robinia pseudoacacia*
Street trees, especially in southern Europe	*Albizia julibrissin*
Native and naturalistic schemes	*Ulex, Genista, Cytisus*
Soil reclamation	*Lupinus arboreus*
Yellow-flowered trees	*Laburnum* and *Sophora*
Yellow-leaved large trees	*Gleditsia triacanthos* 'Sunburst' and *R. pseudoacacia* 'Frisia'
Parkland trees for warmer situations	*Gymnocladus diocus*

GROWING CONDITIONS. Due to the presence of the nitrogen-fixing bacteria *Rhizobium* in root nodules, many species can fix atmospheric nitrogen. This allows the plants to grow in impoverished soils, where they in turn can assist in the development of soil fertility.

Trees enjoy a warmer climate rather than a colder one and many are grown in the south of England and the Mediterranean.

MANAGEMENT. Little pruning is required. *Cytisus* and *Genista* can become straggly and are best removed after a few years.

PARTICULAR PLANTING SCHEMES OR PLANT ASSOCIATIONS. The Laburnum Walk at Bodnant, Wales, is one of many examples of *Laburnum* trained to form covered walkways or arbors.

Cercis, Robinia, Albizia and *Ceratonia* are planted as amenity trees in Greece.

Huge specimens of *Robinia pseudoacacia* occur in parks and gardens in London. Bean (1980) states: 'Perhaps no American tree has made itself so thoroughly at home in Europe as this.' Bean's words have come true on the embankments of motorways in Germany and Greece, where the tree has become naturalized.

Landscape trees from the *Fabaceae*

Cercis siliquastrum. Pink flowers and short seed pods cluster around the stems. Leaves are entire.

Gleditsia triacanthos 'Sunburst', is a large-growing tree with pinnate leaves and, in this cultivar, yellow leaves.

Laburnum alpinum, L. anagyroides, L. × *watereri* 'Vossii'. They are small to medium-sized trees with yellow flowers. Planted together they will appear to be one type of tree but will provide a longer flowering period than if only one species had been planted.

R. pseudoacacia 'Frisia'. It is similar to the *Gleditsia* (above) but smaller-growing. *R. pseudoacacia* 'Umbraculifera' is a small tree with a distinctive globular-shaped head.

Sophora tetraptera is an evergreen medium-sized tree with dark green pinnate leaves and deep yellow flowers, somewhat tubular in shape, and bead-like seed pods.

Landscape climbers

Wisteria sinensis. Mauve flowers borne profusely in early summer, with a second flush in early autumn, particularly in the south-east of England.

Landscape shrubs

Cytisus battendieri. Silver-coloured trifoliate leaves and pineapple-scented flowers develop in early summer. *Cytisus scoparius* and cultivars. Many cultivars of common broom are available, in shades of yellow, burnt orange and pink.

Genista lydia. When in flower, plants are wreathed in yellow flowers. Out of flower, they are a network of twiggy shoots. *G. hispanica.* Low-growing with prickly foliage and yellow flowers. *G. tenera.* A tall shrub with green stems and highly adapted foliage, it has small yellow flowers.

Indigofera heterantha. It is useful for midsummer, when few shrubs are in flower. It has mauve flowers.

Lupinus arboreus. Fast-growing, short-lived shrubs with yellow flowers, but seedlings will self-sow and new plants develop.

Spartium junceum. With rush-like (*Juncus*) foliage and yellow flowers, this shrub is rarely out of bloom.

Ulex europaeus. Yellow, scented flowers and prickly foliage, rarely out of flower.

Native shrubs

Cytisus scoparius. Common broom.
Ulex europaeus. Gorse, furze, whin.
Ulex gallii.

——————————————— • ———————————————

Fagaceae Beech and Oak

Fagus sylvatica (beech) and cultivars, *Castanea sativa* (Spanish/sweet chestnut) and several species of *Quercus* (oak) are widely cultivated in rural and urban situations (Table 4.11). They become large, dome-shaped trees on maturity (Fig. 2.3). *Nothofagus* (southern beech) is limited to collections but has much to recommend it for wider landscape use.

TYPES OF PLANTS. Trees are generally long-lived and large, 20–40 m tall.

WORLD DISTRIBUTION. Temperate regions of northern and southern hemispheres.

LEAVES. Foliage is deciduous or evergreen. Alternate leaves are stalked, entire or lobed with leaf margins, entire or serrated.

FLOWERS. Male flowers are in erect or pendent catkins. When numerous they are conspicuous on the tree, especially in *C. sativa* (yellow catkins), *Quercus ilex* (evergreen oak) (whitish-green catkins) and *Q. cerris* (yellow catkins). Female flowers are solitary or in threes.

FRUIT. Fruit is a nut with one to three seeds partly enclosed, e.g. acorn (*Quercus*), or fully enclosed, e.g. beech mast (*Fagus*), in a cupule.

GROWTH RATE AND LONGEVITY. Growth rate varies with the genus. *Quercus* and *Castanea* are slow-growing and take a number of years to make an impact on their surroundings. However, this impact lasts for 200–300 years. *Fagus* is faster-growing and long-lived, upwards of 200 years. *Nothofagus*, *N. procera* and *N. obliqua* in particular, are very fast-growing some 1.5 m per year.

FUNCTIONAL AND ORNAMENTAL USES.

Parkland trees	*Quercus robur, Q. petraea, Q. cerris and Q. ilex, Fagus sylvatica* and *Castanea sativa.*
Street trees	*Q. robur* f. *fastigiata*
Native woodland	*Q. robur* and *Q. petraea*
Hedges	*Q. ilex* and *F. sylvatica*
Fastigiate trees	*F. sylvatica* 'Dawyck' *Q. robur* f. *fastigiata*
Shelter belts	*Q. ilex*
Autumn colour	*Q. coccinea* and *Q. rubra*

Table 4.11. Principal genera from the *Fagaceae* in cultivation.

Species	Common name	Height (m)	Bark	Foliage	Fruit	Winter buds	Function
Castanea	Spanish chestnut	30	Twisted and angled spirals	Entire, elliptic, margin toothed, veins prominent	Prickly husk encloses 1–2 brown nuts	Bud ovoid	Parkland tree, avenue tree
Fagus	Beech	40	Grey, smooth	Deciduous, entire, silky-hairy when young, good autumn colour	Cupule, prickly on the outside, encloses triangular-shaped nuts	Brown, pointed buds c.1 cm	Parkland tree, street tree (fastigiated forms only)
Nothofagus	Southern beech	15–30	Shallowly fissured	Deciduous and evergreen, alternate, veins conspicuous	Small nut at the base of a leaf	Bud 1 cm, bud tiny in evergreen species	Parkland tree
Quercus	Oak	20–35	Shallowly to deeply fissured	Deciduous and evergreen, entire, toothed or lobed	Acorn nut sits in a woody cupule	Tiny brown buds cluster around tips of shoots	Native woodland, parkland tree, street tree (fastigiated forms only)

GROWING CONDITIONS. *Castanea* is suited to hot dry conditions. *Fagus* will grow on poorer soils. *Quercus* is a pioneer species and will grow on infertile as well as fertile soils.

MANAGEMENT. *Fagus* is shallow-rooted and can be blown over in a storm.

PARTICULAR PLANTING SCHEMES OR PLANT ASSOCIATIONS. There are a number of some 400-year-old pollarded *Q. robur* (oak) at Richmond Park and Windsor Great Park near London. Trees of a similar age are extant at Ashtown Wood, Phoenix Park, Dublin (Fig. 2.2).

A few rows of venerable old specimens of *C. sativa* (sweet chestnut) grow at Greenwich Park, London, remnants of 17th century baroque-style planting.

F. sylvatica (beech) hedges are a feature of the 17th century garden at Killruddery, County Wicklow, Ireland.

Tall, clipped, cylinders of *F. sylvatica* (beech) accentuate the formality of gardens surrounding the Orangery, Kensington Gardens, London.

Large specimens of *F. sylvatica purpurea* (purple beech) and *F. sylvatica* 'Pendula' (weeping beech) occur in many old estates in Britain and Ireland (Fig. 2.1).

Q. coccinea, a North American species, has become naturalized in the Soignes Forest near Brussels and in many parts of Eastern Europe.

Nothofagus (southern beech)

Nothofagus is a southern hemisphere genus of deciduous and evergreen trees, very similar to *Fagus* (beech). *N. procera* is a fast-growing, deciduous, tall, elegant tree with a smooth bark. Evergreen species, such as *N. dombeyi* and *N. antarctica*, are confined to collections but would make attractive park and amenity trees in favoured situations.

Quercus (oak)

Quercus is native to the temperate regions of the world. Foliage is deciduous or evergreen, lobed or entire (Fig. 4.5). Of 18 Mediterranean and western Asian species, two are common in cultivation, *Q. ilex* and *Q. cerris*; of 19 North American species, one, *Q. rubra*, is common and, of eight western North American species and 13 Asiatic species none are common (Forrest, 2004). Of 124 named cultivars, some 40 are cultivated in collections, 33 are available from specialist nurseries and one, *Q. robur* f. *fastigiata*, is widely available (Jablonskii, 2004). Characteristics of *Quercus* (oak) common in cultivation are given in Table 4.12.

Fagus (beech)

Fagus is native in the south of England and in Europe. It has become naturalized in other parts of Britain and Ireland. It is a long-lived tree and

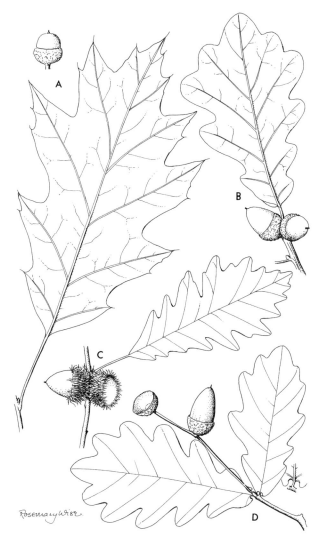

Fig. 4.5. (A) *Quercus rubra*, red oak; (B) *Quercus petraea*, sessile oak; (C) *Quercus cerris*, Turkey oak; (D) *Quercus robur*, pedunculate oak. These show the range of foliage in deciduous *Quercus* species. (From Savill, 1991.)

many fine examples of woodland and parkland trees occur. Many cultivars have been selected (Table 4.13).

In general, purple-leaved, cut-leaved or pendulous forms of trees or shrubs are not as vigorous as the species from which they have derived. However, this is not the case with *F. sylvatica* var. *heterophylla*, *F. sylvatica* 'Pendula' and *F. sylvatica* Atropurpurea Group, which form large parkland trees, as seen in Fig. 2.1.

Table 4.12. Common *Quercus* (oak) in cultivation.

Species	Common name	Height (m)	Foliage	Fruit	Function
Quercus cerris	Turkey oak	35	Deciduous, leaves lobed, twisted whiskers on bud	Acorn, 'mossy' cup	Parkland tree
Quercus ilex	Evergreen/ holm oak	20–25	Evergreen, holly-like on young trees, entire on older trees	Acorn, grey, small	Parkland tree, shelter belt in maritime areas
Quercus petraea	Sessile oak	30–40	Deciduous, base of leaf cuneate	Acorn, sessile, attached directly to shoot	Native woodland, parkland tree
Quercus robur	Pedunculate oak, English oak	35	Deciduous, base of leaf auricled	Acorn, attached to a stalk	Native woodland, parkland tree
Quercus rubra	Red oak	35	Deciduous	Acorn, on short stalk	Parkland tree, amenity tree

Table 4.13. *Fagus sylvatica* and cultivars.

Scientific name	Common name	Form and habit	Foliage	Function
Fagus sylvatica	Beech	Large, dome-shaped	Entire, elliptic, with prominent veins	Parkland tree
F. sylvatica Atropurpurea Group	Copper beech	Large, dome-shaped	As in species but purple	Parkland tree
F. sylvatica 'Dawyck'	Dawyck beech	Upright, fastigiate	As above	Columnar tree for narrow spaces
F. sylvatica var. *heterophylla*	Fern-leaved beech	Large, dome-shaped tree	Foliage variously cut in small and large lobes	Parkland tree
F. sylvatica 'Pendula'	Weeping beech	Large tree with weeping branches	As in species	Parkland tree
F. sylvatica 'Purpurea Pendula'	Weeping copper beech	Small compact weeping tree	As in species but purple	Small, neat tree for a small space

Ginkgoaceae Ginkgo or Maidenhair Tree

One genus with one species is all that remains of this coniferous family, whose ancestors were cosmopolitan in the Jurassic period, 180 million years ago. Once confined to collections, this species is grown as a street tree in parts of Europe. This is one of a number of deciduous conifers, the others being *Larix*, *Taxodium* and *Metasequoia*, which are covered in this book.

TYPES OF PLANTS. Tree: large tree to 25 m. One species, *Ginkgo biloba*, is cultivated.

WORLD DISTRIBUTION. China, now limited in the wild.

LEAVES. Foliage is deciduous, dark green, fan-shaped with noticeable veins. The leaves are shaped like the tiny pinnule (leaf) of a maidenhair fern, hence the common name. Bright yellow autumn colour develops in late October. Foliage emerges from short spur-like growth.

FLOWERS. Male and female inflorescences occur on separate trees.

FRUIT. These are green, ripening to yellow. They have an unpleasant smell as they rot. For this reason, female trees are avoided in street tree planting.

BARK. The bark is corky and fissured when young and deeply fissured when old.

GROWTH RATE AND LONGEVITY. It is fast-growing in some years, with slow or no growth in other years. It is long-lived.

FUNCTIONAL AND ORNAMENTAL USES.
Specimen tree.
Street tree.

GROWING CONDITIONS. *Ginkgo* benefits from a warmer climate. It is grown in the south of England and continental Europe.

MANAGEMENT. Remove shoots that develop at the base of the trunk. Select leader and formatively prune the tree.

PARTICULAR PLANTING SCHEMES OR PLANT ASSOCIATIONS. A specimen planted in the Royal Botanic Gardens, Kew, in 1754 is still growing.
      At first glance, a huge tree by the side of Liechtenstein Palace, Vienna, with deep green, rounded leaves, looked like a *Tilia* (lime), but on further inspection, this tree, with three main trunks and many side branches, was identified as a *Ginkgo*.
      Ginkgo is grown as a street tree in Brussels and Vienna. It tends to send out long single branches and can be rather ungainly as a street tree.
      It is also grown in parks and urban woodland in southern Europe (Saebø *et al.*, 2005).

Hamamelidaceae Witch Hazel

They are very useful ornamental flowering shrubs and trees, usually with excellent autumn colour for well-favoured situations.

TYPES OF PLANTS. Trees: small to medium-sized.
Shrubs: medium to large shrubs.

WORLD DISTRIBUTION. North America, eastern Asia and western Asia.

LEAVES. Foliage is alternate, deciduous in the genera treated here. Leaves are ovate or obovate in shape, and leaf veins are conspicuous in *Hamamelis*, *Corylopsis* and *Fothergilla*. Foliage in *Liquidamber* is long-stalked and the leaf blade is palmately lobed. It can be confused with *Acer* (maple), which has opposite leaves.

FLOWERS. In the deciduous genera flowers are borne on bare wood in winter or early spring. Flower shape and colour vary:

Corylopsis. Flowers are scented in drooping racemes.
Fothergilla. Flowers are white in upright racemes.
Hamamelis (witch hazel). Flowers are scented and petals are strap-like in colours of yellow, orange and reddish orange.
Parrotia. Flowers are highly adapted and red anthers on the tips of shoots are a conspicuous feature.

FRUIT. Fruit is a woody capsule, rarely seen in cultivation.

GROWTH RATE AND LONGEVITY. Growth rate is slow in most genera but they are long-lived. It is a number of years before *Parrotia* begins to blossom.

FUNCTIONAL AND ORNAMENTAL USES.
Winter-flowering shrubs   *Hamamelis, Parrotia*
Spring-flowering shrubs   *Corylopsis*
Autumn colour   spectacular in *Liquidamber, Fothergilla* and
                                        Hamamelis

GROWING CONDITIONS. Good growing conditions, i.e. good soil and a sheltered situation, are required for these genera. They will tolerate low temperatures. *Hamamelis* continue to blossom unscathed by winter snow.
Fothergilla requires acidic soil conditions and is one of the few genera other than members of the *Ericaceae* that require such conditions.
Liquidamber do not grow as well in Western Europe as in the USA.

MANAGEMENT. They require little pruning.

PARTICULAR PLANTING SCHEMES OR PLANT ASSOCIATIONS. The Sir Harold Hillier Arboretum has developed a winter garden in which many of these genera feature.
A wide-spreading specimen of *Parrotia persica* at the entrance of National Botanic Gardens, Glasnevin, Dublin, is underplanted with spring-flowering *Crocus*.

Hippocastanaceae Horse Chestnut

This family comprises two genera, of which one, *Aesculus*, is cultivated. A candle-like inflorescence, digitate (hand-like) foliage and rich brown seed known as 'conkers' are useful clues to the identification of members of this genus.

TYPES OF PLANTS. Trees: medium to large, 30–35m tall, long-lived trees.

Shrubs: One suckering, shrubby, species, *Aesculus parviflora*, with yellow flowers borne in August.

WORLD DISTRIBUTION. Many are native to North America and Europe. *Aesculus hippocastanum* is native to southern Europe but has long been in cultivation in north-western Europe.

LEAVES. Foliage is opposite, with large, digitate (hand-like) leaves, each with five to seven leaflets.

FLOWERS. Panicles of pale white, yellow, pink or reddish flowers are borne in late spring and early summer.

FRUIT. Fruit is green, turning brown, breaking open to reveal a chestnut-brown seed, the 'conker' of children's games.

FUNCTIONAL AND ORNAMENTAL USES.
Parkland trees   *Aesculus hippocastanum*
Park trees in suburban areas   *Aesculus indica*

GROWING CONDITIONS. It will withstand city conditions.

MANAGEMENT. See the section in Chapter 5, Trees: Selection, Use and Management.

PESTS AND DISEASES. Horse chestnut leaf blotch, *Guignardia aesculi*, was recorded in 12 European countries. It causes foliage to become blotched brown and fall prematurely. Horse chestnut leaf miner, *Cameraria ohridella*, was also recorded in 12 countries; it is more common in Eastern Europe than in Western Europe but is spreading rapidly. Larvae feed on the leaves, i.e. mine, causing foliage to brown and die prematurely (Tello *et al.*, 2005). Horse chestnut scale insect, *Pulvinaria regalis*, is also becoming widespread in several European cities. White scales are particularly noticeable on the undersurface of small branches and on the trunks of trees, *Aesculus*, *Acer* and *Tilia* in particular. While not life-threatening to the trees, these diseases and pests debilitate trees that are already growing in difficult conditions.

OTHER. Prominent leaf scars and sticky buds distinguish *A. hippocastanum* from other species and genera.

PARTICULAR PLANTING SCHEMES OR PLANT ASSOCIATIONS. There are magnificent examples of *A. indica* in Kensington Gardens and other London parks resplendent in pink flowers in late June and July.

What could be described as a copse of *A. hippocastanum* is growing in a city square adjacent to the cathedral in Basle, Switzerland, and demonstrates a policy of planting large-growing trees closer to buildings than is the practice in much of Britain and Ireland.

Horse chestnuts are clearly identifiable in Claude Monet's painting of 1866, *Saint Germain L'Auxerrois*, a square in Paris. Horse chestnuts remain common in boulevards in Paris and Brussels.

In the mid-1940s, the 2.5-mile-long 'Long Walk' at Windsor Great Park was replanted with a double row of *Aesculus* and *Platanus*. It is one landscape scheme that is clearly visible as one departs from Heathrow Airport.

The sequence of flowering of common *Aesculus* in cultivation is *A. hippocastanum* May, *Aesculus* × *carnea* Briotii, late May, and *A. indica*, June–early July.

-------------------- • --------------------

Juglandaceae Walnut

While not frequently planted on any scale, many fine examples of *Pterocarya* (wing nut) and *Juglans* (walnut) occur in older estates and public parks, where they become large majestic trees. *Carya* (hickory) is generally confined to collections.

TYPES OF PLANTS. Trees: large parkland, 20–30 m tall.

WORLD DISTRIBUTION. North America, Europe and China.

LEAVES. Large pinnate leaves are characteristic of this family with, depending on the genus and species, five to 21 leaflets per leaf. In *Pterocarya* (wing nut) foliage is up to 60 cm long and the leaf stalk is swollen at the base where it is attached to the shoot, not unlike a ball and socket joint. Pith in the young shoots is a useful tool to distinguish genera. Other distinguishing features are included in Table 4.14.

FLOWERS. Male flowers, borne on catkins 5–10 cm long in May–June, are hidden in the previous year's shoots. Female flowers are in spikes on the current year's new growth. Neither male nor female flowers are particularly ornamental or conspicuous.

FRUIT. A green nut is enclosed by a thick fleshy cover.

BARK. Grey, ridged bark occurs in *Juglans* and *Pterocarya*.

GROWTH RATE AND LONGEVITY. Depending on the species, they vary from slow, e.g. *Juglans regia*, to fast-growing, e.g. *Juglans nigra* and *Pterocarya fraxinifolia*.

Table 4.14. Distinguishing features of genera in *Juglandaceae*.

Genus	Common name	Pith[a]	Number of leaflets	Fruit
Carya	Hickory	Continuous	4–9 leaflets, entire	Large nut, 2–3 together
Juglans	Walnut	Chambered	3–9 leaflets, entire (*Juglans regia*), 11–12 leaflets serrated (*Juglans nigra*)	Globose with a thick, green seed coat
Pterocarya	Wing nut	Chambered	5–27 leaflets to 60 cm, flaccid in appearance	Small winged nut in long pendent spikes

[a] To examine the pith, cut a twig at an oblique angle and remove a length of bark; the pith is then visible.

FUNCTIONAL AND ORNAMENTAL USES.

Specimen tree for large-scale situations	*Pterocarya fraxinifolia*
Avenue tree	*Juglans*

GROWING CONDITIONS. They thrive in warmer situations, as in the south of England and on the European mainland.

MANAGEMENT. As *Juglans* 'weep' sap when pruned, pruning is undertaken in summer when it has least effect on the tree.

Pterocarya tends to sucker and should be grown in a situation where suckers around the base of a tree are not a problem.

PARTICULAR PLANTING SCHEMES OR PLANT ASSOCIATIONS. There are several large specimens of *P. fraxinifolia* (wing nut) in the Englischer Garten, Munich, Germany. There are also fine examples in Powerscourt, County Wicklow, and Talbot Botanic Gardens, Malahide, County Dublin, Ireland.

In University College Dublin many *J. regia* are self-sown on the campus.

———————————— • ————————————

Lamiaceae Dead Nettle or Mint

This family includes shrubs and many subshrubs, perennial plants and the commercial herb plants *Mentha* (mint), *Thymus* (thyme) and *Lavandula* (lavender). Many are clothed in soft hairs and oil glands, providing both a tactile and an aromatic quality. A square stem, opposite leaves and a zygomorphic flower distinguish this family from other families.

TYPES OF PLANTS. Shrubs: small to medium-sized shrubs.

WORLD DISTRIBUTION. Distribution is cosmopolitan but with a concentration of species in the Mediterranean region.

LEAVES. Foliage is opposite leaves, generally scented and soft to the touch. The stem is generally square in outline. Leaves vary in size from broadly elliptic in *Phlomis* to linear in *Lavandula* (lavender) and *Rosmarinus* (rosemary). The leaves and stem are often clothed in dense hairs, e.g. *Phlomis* and *Ballota*. Due to the presence of oil glands in the leaves, many of these shrubs are known for their scent. Table 4.15 outlines the key characteristics of *Lamiaceae*.

FLOWERS. Flowers are borne singly, in whorls or racemes. Each flower is zygomorphic, i.e. bilaterally symmetrical; if one is to bisect the flower to give two equal parts, it can only be done in one way. Each flower is tubular with two lips occurring at the apex of the tube; the upper lip is two-lobed and often hooded and the lower three-lobed, providing a landing platform for insects. Flower colour varies from blue, pink or yellow to mauve, red or purple.

FRUIT. One or four dry nutlets develop, but they are small and not of ornamental importance.

GROWTH RATE AND LONGEVITY. Fast-growing, short-lived shrubs, 5–10–15 years.

FUNCTIONAL AND ORNAMENTAL USES.
Shrubberies in maritime areas and in dry sunny situations.
    Grey foliage borders.
    Herb gardens.

GROWING CONDITIONS. They will grow in a variety of soils, though damp soils should be avoided. As they are native to the Mediterranean, they are suitable for dry, hot, baked conditions. Given that many shrubs are clothed in hairs, they can withstand the high light conditions often prevalent in cities, where light is reflected from pavements and buildings.

MANAGEMENT. Shrubs can be pruned severely and will regenerate. Where shrubs have not been pruned for many years and they have become woody, it is

Table 4.15. Key characteristics of shrubby genera in the *Lamiaceae*.

Name	Size	Foliage	Flower	Function
Ballota pseudodictnamus	75 cm	Round leaves, very densely clothed in hairs	Pink, in whorls	Ground cover for a dry site
Lavandula	50–75 cm	Linear, grey	Blue, pink, white	Scented shrub, hedge
Phlomis fruticosa	1–2 m	Elliptic, densely clothed in hairs	Yellow	
Rosmarinus officinalis	1–2 m	Linear, grey	Blue	Scented shrub
Salvia officinalis	75 cm–1 m	Long, stalked, green	Purple	Herb
Teucrium chamaedrys	50 cm	Green	Pink	Edging shrub
Teucrium fruticans	1.5 m	Grey	Pale blue	Maritime shrubbery

advisable to prune some branches in one year and, once new shoots have developed, to prune further branches in subsequent years. In the case of very woody specimens of *Lavandula*, it would be advisable to remove and replant.

PARTICULAR PLANTING SCHEMES OR PLANT ASSOCIATIONS. *Phlomis fruticosa* is a large-growing shrub with yellow flowers, suitable for landscape situations where soil is dry. In well-favoured situations in the south-east of England, *Phlomis italica* grows well.

The specimen of *Rosmarinus officinalis* Prostratus Group cultivated on the campus of University College Dublin has formed a wide-spreading, dense ground cover and is rarely without pale blue flowers.

Salvia microphylla var. *microphylla* grows in gardens in inner London. Many tender Mexican and South American *Salvia* species are becoming more common in cultivation.

-------------------------------- • --------------------------------

Magnoliaceae Magnolia and Tulip Tree

They are long-lived flowering trees for milder locations.

TYPES OF PLANTS. Trees: 20–30 m.
Shrubs: wide-spreading shrubby trees.

WORLD DISTRIBUTION. Eastern North America, Himalaya, China.

LEAVES. Foliage is evergreen or deciduous, with alternate leaves. In *Magnolia* the developing leaf bud is narrow and convolute (rolled in on itself). In *Liriodendron* the bud is conduplicate (flattened like a piece of notepaper). Large elliptic leaves occur in the larger-growing tree *Magnolia*, with narrow, lanceolate leaves in the shrubby species and cultivars. In *Liriodendron* the adult foliage is truncated: imagine a maple leaf, 'square it off' by removing the lobes, and that is the shape of a *Liriodendron*.

FLOWERS. In *Magnolia* the flower buds are conspicuous, cone-shaped, enclosed in hairy bracts, which are velvet-like to the touch. In the deciduous species of *Magnolia*, flowers are borne on bare wood or as the leaves emerge. In the evergreen species, they bloom intermittently over the summer months. Flowers are solitary, with six to nine tepals (petals and sepals are not distinguishable from one another and are known as tepals). In *Liriodendron*, pale yellow flowers emerge in June and July. They are shaped like a tulip; hence the common name tulip tree.

FRUIT. Cone-like fruit, often likened to a small cucumber or gherkin, occurs on the tree-sized species. The fruit colour is red, with orange seed within.

BARK. It is generally smooth in *Magnolia* and *Liriodendron*.

GROWTH RATE AND LONGEVITY. *Magnolia* is slow-growing. *Liriodendron* is fast-growing and long-lived, up to 200 years. Both genera can be slow to begin to produce flowers but it is well worth the wait.

FUNCTIONAL AND ORNAMENTAL USES.

Large shrubs for late spring/early summer	*Magnolia* × *soulangeana*
Small sheltered area	*M. stellata, M.* 'Susan' and other small-growing species and cultivars
Fragrant flowers	*M. grandiflora*

Ornamental trees and large shrubs (except *M. stellata*) for well-sheltered situations.

Liriodendron tulipifera is an ideal commemorative tree. Striking in appearance and fast-growing, it will outlive others at a tree-planting ceremony by a great many years.

GROWING CONDITIONS. They need sheltered conditions and a rich, well-drained soil in a semi-woodland situation. *M. grandiflora* will grow in an open sunny situation or against a large wall.

MANAGEMENT. They have thick fleshy roots and do not like root disturbance. They are well worth seeking out for a well-sheltered situation where one can wait for the trees to mature and start to flower. Shrubby magnolias, e.g. *M. stellata* and hybrid magnolias, e.g. *M.* 'Susan', are much more floriferous.

PARTICULAR PLANTING SCHEMES OR PLANT ASSOCIATIONS. *Magnolia* × *soulangeana* is often seen in suburban gardens and parks in Britain and Ireland. In late spring their tulip-shaped flowers in shades of white, pink or purple bridge the gap between spring- and summer-flowering shrubs.

Specimens of *M. grandiflora* are cultivated as free-standing specimens at the Escorial Palace, near Madrid, Spain. It is often container-grown in basement gardens in inner London, where it enjoys the protection of the surrounding buildings.

Many large specimens of *Liriodendron tulipifera* can be seen in old estates in Britain and Ireland. Some fine examples of younger trees occur in a public park in Winchester, England. An avenue of *Liriodendron* planted in Kensington Gardens is reaching maturity.

Malvaceae Mallow and Hibiscus

This family provides tender flowering shrubs and small trees for sheltered coastal and inner-city locations. Flowers are striking, with five petals and conspicuous protruding stamens that have united into a column.

TYPES OF PLANTS. Trees: shrubby trees to 10 m.
   Shrubs: small to medium.

WORLD DISTRIBUTION. Chile, South America, New Zealand and southern France.

LEAVES. In *Lavatera* and *Abutilon* foliage is lobed with conspicuous palmate venation. They have some similarity to the foliage of *Acer* but differ in being clothed in stellate (star-like) hairs. Foliage in *Hoheria* is also slightly hairy, with simple leaves that are variously toothed.

FLOWERS. Flowers have five petals, with five or more conspicuous stamens and five or more conspicuous stigmas and styles. Flower colour varies from white and yellow to pink and purple. The petals have the delicacy of a *Papaver rhoes* (red poppy) but are more trumpet-like in shape.

FRUIT. Depending on the genus, fruit is a capsule or a mericarp. A mericarp, a doughnut-shaped fruit, surrounded by a ring of sepals, occurs in *Abutilon* and *Lavatera*, intriguing rather than picturesque.

GROWTH RATE AND LONGEVITY. *Abutilon*, *Lavatera* and *Hibiscus* are short-lived shrubs, 10–15 years. *Hoheria* is longer-lived.

FUNCTIONAL AND ORNAMENTAL USES.
Ornamental shrubs for well-favoured   *Abutilon, Lavatera* and *Hibiscus*
   situations
Flowering tree for sheltered garden   *Hoheria*

GROWING CONDITIONS. Sheltered sites, good soil.

MANAGEMENT. The shrubby species can become leggy and gaunt and benefit from regular pruning. Prune flowering shoots after flowering.

PARTICULAR PLANTING SCHEMES OR PLANT ASSOCIATIONS. Species and cultivars worth seeking for cultivation in well-favoured situations:

   Abutilon x suntense 'Jermyns'. Early summer-flowering.
   Abutilon vitifolium 'Veronica Tennant'. Early summer-flowering.
   Hibicus syriacus. Late summer-flowering in shades of pink, purple or red, depending on the cultivar.
   Hoheria populnea. White, late summer-flowering, large shrub or small tree with ovate leaves and white flowers. (*Hoheria* is native to New Zealand.)

Hoheria sexstylosa White, late summer-flowering, large shrub or small tree with narrow leaves and small flowers.

Lavatera × clementii 'Barnsley' is a popular medium-sized summer-flowering shrub with many pink flowers. It is suitable for maritime areas.

_____ • _____

Myrtaceae Myrtle

A family of trees and shrubs once confined to warmer parts of Britain and Ireland but now more widespread. *Eucalyptus* is frequently planted in shelter belts in maritime areas. Some genera, such as *Myrtus* (myrtle) and *Metrosideros*, are becoming more common as specimen plants and landscape shrubs for favoured situations. Flowers with a great many stamens and a woody fruit capsule indicate a member of this family (Table 4.16).

TYPES OF PLANTS. Trees: small to medium to large trees.
   Shrubs: small to medium to large.

WORLD DISTRIBUTION. New Zealand, Australia, South America and Europe.

LEAVES. Foliage is opposite, evergreen, often leathery to the touch. Many have scented leaves, in particular *Eucalyptus* and *Myrtus*.

Table 4.16. Distinguishing characteristics of common genera of *Myrtaceae*.

Name	Size (m)	Foliage	Flower	Fruit
Callistemon	1–5	Alternate foliage	Inflorescence a cylindrical spike around a shoot with inconspicuous corolla and very conspicuous stamens in shades of red or yellow.	Woody capsule
Eucalyptus	10–40	Opposite, elliptic to sickle-shaped, green or glaucous green	In clusters of 3, 7 or more, white or yellowish flowers with numerous stamens	Woody capsule
Leptospermum	2–4	Leaves tiny, alternate	White, pink, red	Woody capsule
Lophomyrtus × ralphii		Leaves leathery	4 petals	Berry
Luma apiculata	2–5	Leaves leathery, elliptic	Cup-shaped flowers with 4 white petals	Berry
Metrosideros umbellatus	2	Leathery, elliptic-shaped leaves	5 red petals and numerous stamens	Capsule
Myrtus communis 'Tarentina'	1–2	Small, shiny leaves	4 white petals and many stamens	Berry
Ugni moliniae	1	Leaves opposite, leathery	Solitary flowers, 5 petals, many stamens	Berry

FLOWERS. Stamens are numerous and the calyx and corolla may or may not be conspicuous.

FRUIT. Fruit is a berry, e.g. *Ugni,* or a woody capsule, e.g. *Eucalyptus* and *Callistemon.*

BARK. Peeling stringy bark is noticeable in *Eucalyptus.* The bark of *Luma apiculata* is a burnished brown-red colour.

GROWTH RATE AND LONGEVITY. They are long-lived trees and shrubs and, where favourable conditions occur, they achieve a large size.
Eucalyptus is very fast-growing.

FUNCTIONAL AND ORNAMENTAL USES.

Attractive foliage plants	*Metrosideros*
Shelter belts in well-favoured maritime areas	*Eucalytpus, Luma*
Hedge and topiary	*Myrtus communis*
Grey-foliaged trees/shrubs	*Eucalyptus gunnii* and *E. globulus*
Variegated shrubs	*Luma apiculata* 'Glanleam'

GROWING CONDITIONS. They prefer warm situations and will withstand dry conditions.

MANAGEMENT. *Eucalyptus* are best planted when only a few centimetres tall. If they have been in pots for some time and have attained a few metres in height, the roots will have encircled the pots in which they were growing. When such plants are planted into soil, the roots continue to grow in an encircling manner and the plants will not establish in their new conditions and will be blown over in the wind. Once established for a few years, *Eucalyptus* can be coppiced to within a few centimetres of ground level and will regenerate.

Other members of the genus require little pruning, and it is necessary only when shrubs outgrow their allotted space.

PARTICULAR PLANTING SCHEMES OR PLANT ASSOCIATIONS. Large specimens of *Metrosideros umbellatus* occur at Mount Stewart, County Down, and Glenveagh Castle, County Donegal, Ireland. An evergreen shrub, with polished, dark green, elliptic leaves, it is spectacular in flower, each flower a mass of red stamens. Even if it never flowered, it is an attractive shrub for a well-sheltered seaside garden or an inner-city courtyard.

At Glanleam, a garden on Valentia Island, County Kerry, where *Luma apiculata* has become naturalized, a variegated myrtle was noticed by the owner, propagated and is now named *L. apiculata* 'Glanleam'. Both the species and the cultivar are widely available in the trade.

Myrtus communis is used to create low-growing formal hedges in a parterre-style garden adjacent to the Tower of Belem on the Avenida de Brasilia, Lisbon.

---   •   ---

Oleaceae Olive

This family provides several genera of importance in landscape design – *Fraxinus* (q.v.), *Jasminum* (q.v.), *Ligustrum* (q.v.), *Osmanthus* (q.v.) and *Syringa* (q.v.) (Table 4.17).

Olea europaea (olive) is cultivated as a crop in regions of the world with a Mediterranean climate. In recent years it has become more common in Britain and Ireland as an evergreen shrub for patio gardens in urban situations.

TYPES OF PLANTS. Trees: Medium to large, long-lived.
Shrubs: Small to medium to large.
Climbers: to many metres.

WORLD DISTRIBUTION. Cosmopolitan; many genera occur in eastern Asia.

LEAVES. Foliage is usually opposite without stipules, simple, trifoliate, pinnate, often entire or lobed, deciduous or evergreen.

FLOWERS. The corolla (fused petals) is four-lobed, white, yellow or lilac. Some flowers are scented. A corolla is absent in *Fraxinus excelsior* (ash), but reddish/purple stamens and stigmas are conspicuous.

Table 4.17. Genera from the *Oleaceae* commonly cultivated in landscape schemes.

Genus	Tree	Shrub	Climber	Leaves	D	E	Flower colour	Scent	Time of flowering	Fruit
Forsythia		x		Entire	x		Yellow		Spring	
Fraxinus	x			Pinnate	x		Red/purple, white		Spring, early summer	Green then turning to brown samara
Jasminum		x	x	Pinnate		x	White/ yellow/ pink	Sweet	Winter, summer	
Ligustrum	x	x		Entire		x	White	Musty	Summer	Black
Osmanthus		x		Entire		x	White	Sweet	Spring,	
Syringa		x		Usually entire	x		Lilac, pink, white, single, double	Sweet	early summer	

D, deciduous foliage; E, evergreen foliage.

FRUIT. Various kinds of fruit occur, capsule, berry, drupe, nut or samara. The fruit may be dry (*Fraxinus*) or fleshy (*Olea* (olive)).

GROWTH RATE AND LONGEVITY. They are fast-growing and long-lived. *Fraxinus excelsior* lives for *c.*200 years. *Ligustrum* (privet), *Syringa* (lilac) and *Jasminum nudiflorum* (winter jasmine) survive in suburban gardens and parks for many years.

FUNCTIONAL AND ORNAMENTAL USES.

Parkland trees	*Fraxinus excelsior* (ash), *F. ornus* (manna ash)
Native and naturalistic schemes	*F. excelsior* and *Ligustrum vulgare*
Ornamental specimen trees	*F. excelsior* 'Pendula' (weeping ash) and *F. ornus* (manna ash)
Shrubberies and hedges	*Ligustrum*
Scented climbers	*Jasminum* (jasmine)
Flowering shrubs	*Forsythia* and *Syringa vulgaris* (lilac) provide striking seasonal interest in spring and early summer, respectively

GROWING CONDITIONS. They can be cultivated in a variety of soils.

MANAGEMENT. They require little pruning, except for *Forsythia* and those grown as hedges. Shrubs will tolerate severe pruning.

For trees see the section in Chapter 5, Trees: Selection, Use and Management.

PARTICULAR PLANTING SCHEMES OR PLANT ASSOCIATIONS. See individual entries below.

Fraxinus (ash)

TYPES OF PLANTS. Trees.

WORLD DISTRIBUTION. Native to the northern hemisphere.

LEAVES. Foliage is deciduous pinnate. A squat angled bud distinguishes them from other trees throughout the year (Fig. 4.6).

FLOWERS. White petals in *Fraxinus ornus*. Reddish/purple stamens and stigmas are distinctive on *Fraxinus excelsior* (ash).

FRUIT. Bunches of green and then brown seed (samara) are held long into the winter.

BARK. Grey, smooth bark occurs on young trees, becoming rough and fissured as trees mature.

GROWTH RATE AND LONGEVITY. Long-lived, up to 200 years.

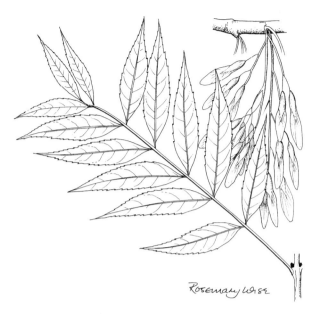

Fig. 4.6. *Fraxinus excelsior*, ash. (From Savill, 1991.)

FUNCTIONAL AND ORNAMENTAL USES.

Ornamental flowering tree	*F. ornus* (manna ash)
Native and naturalistic	*F. excelsior*
Landscape trees in industrial areas	*F. excelsior*

GROWING CONDITIONS. *Fraxinus* is a sparsely leaved and branched tree so a lot of vegetation can live beneath it. It grows on a variety of soils but grows best in a well-drained soil.

MANAGEMENT. See the section in Chapter 5, Trees: Selection, Use and Management.

PARTICULAR PLANTING SCHEMES OR PLANT ASSOCIATIONS. *F. ornus* (manna ash) is a very ornamental tree in late spring and early summer when other trees have gone out of flower.

    Fraxinus (ash) is native, with self-sown seedlings. A weeping ash (*F. excelsior* 'Pendula') was a feature of many Victorian and Edwardian gardens. Venerable old specimens occur in old gardens.

    On the campus of University College, Dublin, *Quercus ilex* (evergreen oak) and *F. excelsior* 'Jaspidea' are planted together to form a barrier planting. The *Q. ilex* acts as a foil for the orange/yellow trunks of *F. excelsior* 'Jaspidea', while the dark, sombre foliage of *Quercus* is lightened by the billowing foliage of *Fraxinus*.

Jasminum (jasmine)

TYPES OF PLANTS. Shrubs: medium.
Climbers: to several metres.

WORLD DISTRIBUTION. Himalaya, China.

LEAVES. Evergreen leaves are opposite, either simple, trifoliate or pinnate.

FLOWERS. Tubular calyx and the corolla is coloured yellow, white or deep pink. Flowers are often sweetly scented.

FRUIT. Not seen in cultivation.

GROWTH RATE AND LONGEVITY. Climbing species can become rampant. Shrubs are long-lived.

FUNCTIONAL AND ORNAMENTAL USES. Climbing species attach themselves by scrambling over trellises or other shrubs.
Winter-flowering shrub: *Jasminum nudiflorum* is a hardy dependable shrub with yellow flowers borne on bare wood in winter.

GROWING CONDITIONS. Climbing species, e.g. *Jasminum officinale* and *J.* × *stephanense*, can be very vigorous. If cultivated for their flower and scent they should be planted in poorer rather than richer soil.
Some species can be defoliated by severe frost but will leaf out in summer.

MANAGEMENT. In a favourable location, climbing species may require severe pruning every few years.

Ligustrum (privet)

TYPES OF PLANTS. Shrubs: medium to large.

WORLD DISTRIBUTION. China, Japan, Europe.

LEAVES. Foliage is evergreen or semi-evergreen, matt to glossy green and glabrous. Some variegated cultivars have been selected.

FLOWERS. Flowers are borne in terminal panicles on side shoots; they are white with a musty smell.

FRUIT. Black drupes are inconspicuous on the plant.

GROWTH RATE AND LONGEVITY. They are fast-growing and long-lived.

FUNCTIONAL AND ORNAMENTAL USES.

Hedge	*Ligustrum ovalifolium*
Medium- to large-sized shrubs for landscape schemes	
Native and naturalistic schemes	*Ligustrum vulgare* is native in Britain
Variegated shrubs	*L. ovalifolium* 'Aureum', *L. lucidum* 'Excelsum Superbum'

GROWING CONDITIONS. *L. ovalifolium* and *L. vulgare* are suited to less favoured sites, whereas some species, e.g. *L. lucidum*, prefer a warmer climate and are planted in southern England.

MANAGEMENT. Hedges: trim once or twice a year. An *L. ovalifolium* (privet) hedge can be pruned to bare wood and will regenerate.

PARTICULAR PLANTING SCHEMES OR PLANT ASSOCIATIONS. Many hedges of *L. ovalifolium* (privet) planted in the 1940s and 1950s in Dublin remain extant and in good condition.

    L. lucidum develops conspicuous panicles of white flowers in July. It is commonly planted in Italy. A variegated form of *L. lucidum* is grown as a street tree in central London.

Osmanthus

TYPES OF PLANTS. Shrubs: medium-sized.

WORLD DISTRIBUTION. China, Japan.

LEAVES. Evergreen leaves are opposite, with entire leaves or armed with spines.

FLOWERS. Flowers are axillary, often hidden by foliage; some are sweetly scented.

FRUIT. Not a noticeable feature.

GROWTH RATE AND LONGEVITY. They are slow-growing and long-lived.

FUNCTIONAL AND ORNAMENTAL USES.

Evergreen shrub for landscape situations	*Osmanthus heterophyllus*
Evergreen flowering shrub	*O. delavayi*
Neat dense hedge	*O. decorus*

GROWING CONDITIONS. They grow well in most soils. As they flower in spring, frost pockets should be avoided.

MANAGEMENT. If they grow too large for their location, they can be pruned, but they are slower- rather than faster-growing shrubs.

PARTICULAR PLANTING SCHEMES OR PLANT ASSOCIATIONS. *O. heterophyllus* can be confused with *Ilex aquifolium* (holly). Foliage is opposite in *Osmanthus* and alternate in *Ilex*.

Syringa (lilac)

TYPES OF PLANTS. Shrubs or shrubby trees.

WORLD DISTRIBUTION. Eastern Europe, but most *Syringa* cultivated are of garden origin.

LEAVES. Foliage is entire, simple, matt green, ovate or heart-shaped in the most commonly seen *Syringa vulgaris*. A pinnate-leaved species, *Syringa pinnatifolia*, is confined to collections.

FLOWERS. Many individual flowers are held in terminal or lateral paniculate-cymose clusters. Flowers are scented.

FRUIT. Rarely seen in cultivation.

GROWTH RATE AND LONGEVITY. Easy to establish and long-lived.

FUNCTIONAL AND ORNAMENTAL USES. Shrubberies in urban areas and scented shrubs.

GROWING CONDITIONS. They are tough, hardy plants, long cultivated in urban parks and gardens.

MANAGEMENT. After flowering, prune flowering wood. They can be severely pruned but this can result in loss of flower for one season. *Syringa* tends to sucker and suckers can be removed in winter.

PARTICULAR PLANTING SCHEMES OR PLANT ASSOCIATIONS. *Syringa vulgaris* was widely planted in urban gardens, and many large billowing shrubs produce lilac, white or purple flowers in May and June.

   Syringa × *josiflexa* 'Bellicent' is less common and less showy than *S. vulgaris*. Superficially it is similar in flower to *Buddleja davidii* (butterfly bush) but it flowers in the early summer rather than early autumn.

   Lilac time is known by many Bostonians as the time to visit the Lilac Walk in the Arnold Arboretum.

Pinaceae Pine, Cedar and Larch

They are coniferous trees with needle-like foliage and conspicuous cones.

Generally medium- to large-sized, venerable, long-lived trees, they are suitable for planting on a large scale or as specimen trees. Some species and cultivars of *Pinus* and *Abies* are suitable for smaller spaces. Some trees have a distinctive triangular shape and regular branching pattern, such as *Picea omorika* (Serbian spruce) (Fig. 2.6). In *Larix* (larch) the branches are semi-pendulous (Fig. 2.14).

TYPES OF PLANTS. Trees: small to medium to large trees.

WORLD DISTRIBUTION. Japan, China, Europe and western North America.

LEAVES. Needle-like foliage is characteristic of the family. In the *Pinus* genus, needles are in bundles of two or three to five, united at the base within a paper-like sheath. In *Cedrus* and *Larix*, foliage is arranged in tufts. In *Abies* and *Picea*, the manner in which foliage is arranged on the shoot varies; sometimes it radiates around the shoot, is parted beneath the shoot or arranged in comb-like ranks above the shoot. In some foliage the needles are sharply pointed at the apex and in others they are rounded. Foliage is often scented. Foliage colour varies from light to glaucous to dark green. The undersurface of the needles, or the inner surface in the case of *Pinus*, is often whitened, with conspicuous bands of stomata. In *Abies* buds are generally clothed in resin. Distinguishing characteristics of foliage in this family are given in Table 4.18.

FLOWERS. Male strobili (i.e. flowers) are borne in 'catkins' of varying lengths. Pale yellow in some species and red in others, they provide some ornamental interest for a short period.

FRUIT. Cones vary in shape from thin elongated to short barrel-shaped. Some are bluish-coloured, e.g. *Abies delavayi*, while those of *Cedrus deodara* are grey and many of the *Pinus* have brownish-coloured cones. Some species cone more readily than others, and few genera cone when trees are in a young state. Even within a particular genus the shape of cone can vary (Fig. 4.7).

BARK. Mature *Pinus*, in particular, develop striking bark patterns, not only in texture but also in colour. Bark colour can be a useful tool in the identification of large trees, as branches are well out of reach even of the longest long-handled pruners. Pointers for the identification of large mature members of the *Pinaceae* are given in Table 4.19.

GROWTH RATE AND LONGEVITY. Initially they are fast-growing and they are often very long-lived. The shape of many conifers changes as the tree matures and develops. *Pinus* are bush-like in habit when young and in maturity become broad, umbrella-shaped trees, for example, in *Pinus sylvestris* (Fig. 2.4). If conifers are grown in close association with one another, as in woodland or forestry, they grow tall and shed their lower branches. Where they are grown as free-standing specimen trees, their statuesque form is very apparent.

Table 4.18. Main differentiating features of commonly planted *Pinaceae*.

Name	Common name	Foliage	Cone	Function
Abies	Fir	Evergreen, needle-like attached to the stem by a sucker pad. When leaves fall, a disc-like scar remains	Erect, shedding their seed from the tree	Specimen tree in collections, ground cover, forestry
Cedrus	Cedar	Evergreen, needle-like, scattered on new young growth, tufted on side shoots	Barrel-shaped, sitting on the shoot	Specimen tree
Larix	Larch	Deciduous, needle-like, scattered on new young growth, tufted on side shoots	Many small barrel-shaped cones sit on top of the branches	Mixed woodland, motorway planting schemes
Picea	Spruce	Evergreen, needle-like, attached to the stem by a short peg. When the needles fall, these pegs remain and the stem is rough to the touch	Cones are pendulous and they fall to the ground	Specimen trees in collections, forestry
Pinus	Pine	Evergreen, needle-like, in bundles of 2, 3 or 5	Woody cones often held on the tree for many years	Shelter, specimen trees, ground cover
Pseudotsuga	Douglas fir	Evergreen, similar to *Abies* but softer to the touch and without the conspicuous leaf scars. Bud like that of *Fagus sylvatica* (beech)	Pendulous cone with conspicuous bracts	Specimen tree in collections, forestry
Tsuga	Hemlock	Evergreen, soft to the touch, leaves of mixed lengths, often twisted to reveal the undersurface of the leaf	Cones small, round or ovoid, hanging from the tips of shoots	Specimens in collections, urban tree, forestry

FUNCTIONAL AND ORNAMENTAL USES.

Naturalistic and native planting schemes	e.g. *Pinus sylvestris, P. nigra, Larix decidua*
Ground cover	e.g. *Pinus mugo* 'Mops'
Shelter belts	e.g. *Pinus radiata, P. sylvestris*
Specimen trees – parkland	*Cedrus atlantica* Glauca Group, *Abies procera*
– small-scale	*Abies koreana* (cones on young trees), *Pinus parviflora*
Forestry tree	e.g. *Picea sitchensis, A. procera, Pseudotsuga menziesii*

GROWING CONDITIONS. They are well adapted to exposed and windy habitats of northern temperate regions. Some *Picea, Abies* and two–three-needled *Pinus* will grow in windswept conditions. Five-needled pines, e.g. *Pinus montezumae* and *Pinus wallichiana*, are more tender than two–three-needled *Pinus* and require a well-sheltered site. Mediterranean species, such as *Pinus halepensis*, grow in hot, dry conditions.

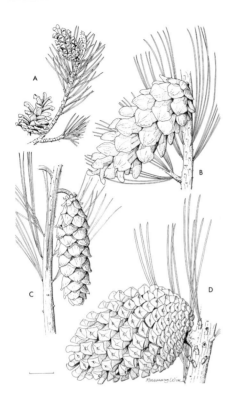

Fig. 4.7. (A) *Pinus sylvestris*, Scots pine; (B) *Pinus peuce*, Macedonian pine; (C) *Pinus strobus*, Weymouth pine; (D) *Pinus radiata*, Monterey pine. (From Savill, 1991.)

MANAGEMENT. Little pruning is required. They cannot be pruned on older wood and will not regenerate.

PARTICULAR PLANTING SCHEMES OR PLANT ASSOCIATIONS. In maritime areas, shelter belts of *Pinus radiata* were commonly planted but in more recent years they have been replaced by × *Cupressocyparis leylandii*.

Cedrus atlantica and *C. deodara* are signatures of late 19th- early 20th-century planting schemes.

Avenues are generally planted with one species. However, at St Anne's Park, Clontarf, Dublin, a mile-long avenue is lined with 100-year-old *P. radiata*, *P. nigra* and *Quercus ilex*.

At the present time *Picea* and *Abies* are more common in landscape schemes in Eastern and Northern Europe and, to a lesser extent, in Mediterranean Europe than in Western Europe.

An examination of regions of origin of the *Pinaceae* in cultivation in urban areas in Europe (Table 4.20) reveals that, in Southern Europe, with the exception of *C. deodara*, which is native to the Himalaya, species are native to the Mediterranean region. In Central Europe many species are

Table 4.19. Identification of large mature members of the *Pinaceae*.

The following are some hints on the identification of *Pinaceae* from a distance:

In old estates *Abies alba* are among the tallest trees peeping up over everything else, often with a secondary leader because the original was blown out. The only other very tall conifer is *Sequoiadendron giganteum*, which has a spire-like outline to the tree.

Orange bark in the upper crown of the tree is a feature of *Pinus sylvestris* and *Pinus halepensis* (common in the Mediterranean).

Pale grey, coarsely ridged bark and a gaunt open crown on maturity is a feature of *Pinus nigra*.

Massive trees with heavy branches, dark green foliage and dark brown rugged corky bark distinguish *Pseudotsuga menziesii* from other species.

Cedrus atlantica Glauca Group is the only glaucous-leaved tree to reach a large size.

Dome-shaped trees, dense crown and dark green foliage are a hallmark of *Pinus pinea* (stone pine).

The cones of *Pinus radiata* (Monterey pine) remain on the tree for many years. Looking up into the crown of a tree one can see whorls of large cones encircling the branches.

Table 4.20. *Pinaceae* in streets, parks and urban woodland in Europe (from Saebø *et al.*, 2005).

Southern Europe	Central Europe	Northern Europe
	Abies alba	*Abies alba*
Abies cephalonica		
	Abies concolor	
	Abies nordmanniana	*Abies nordmanniana*
		Abies sibirica
Cedrus atlantica		*Abies veitchii*
Cedrus deodara		*Larix decidua*
Cedrus libani		*Larix sibirica*
	Picea abies	*Picea abies*
	Picea omorika	*Picea omorika*
	Picea pungens Glauca Group	
	Picea sitchensis	*Picea sitchensis*
Pinus brutia		
		Pinus cembra
Pinus halepensis		
	Pinus heldreichii	
Pinus nigra	*Pinus nigra*	
		Pinus peuce
Pinus pinaster		
Pinus pinea		
	Pinus strobus	
	Pinus sylvestris	*Pinus sylvestris*
	Pseudotsuga menziesii	
	Tsuga canadensis	

native to Europe but several are native to North America; *Abies concolor, Picea pungens* Glauca Group, *Picea sitchensis* and *Pseudotsuga menziesii* are native to western North America and *Pinus strobus* and *Tsuga canadensis* to eastern North America. In Northern Europe the species cultivated are native to that region, with the exception of *Abies veitchii*, native to Japan, and *P. sitchensis*, native to western North America.

Platanaceae Plane

Planes are identified by their *Acer*-like (maple) foliage, which is alternate rather than opposite. Two planes are commonly cultivated, *Platanus × hispanica* in Central and Southern Europe and *P. orientalis* in south-eastern Europe, where it is native. It was widely planted as street and park trees in 19th-century London. This practice continues in many cities. It is described as a 'much used' tree in Central and Southern Europe (Saebø *et al.*, 2005).

TYPES OF PLANTS. Trees: large, 30–40 m tall, with a round, densely branched crown.

WORLD DISTRIBUTION. Native to North America and Southern Europe to India.

LEAVES. Foliage is deciduous, alternate, long-stalked, shaped like an *Acer* (maple) leaf, with usually five main lobes. Alternate leaves, firmer to the touch, distinguish *Platanus* from *Acer*, which has opposite leaves. *Platanus* are later 'into leaf' than similar large trees, but are also late 'out of leaf'. They display little or no autumn colour.

FLOWERS. Male and female catkins are borne on separate trees.

FRUIT. Round fruit, a cluster of achenes, are borne on long stalks. Fruit are noticeable on trees cultivated in London and in continental Europe.

BARK. Large flakes of bark, peeling off to reveal a paler bark beneath, are noticeable on young to middle-aged trees. The bole of older trees becomes burred and 'knobbly'.

GROWTH RATE AND LONGEVITY. They are fast-growing, long-lived trees, often living for 200–300 years.

FUNCTIONAL AND ORNAMENTAL USES. Shade trees, street trees and avenue trees.

GROWING CONDITIONS. They are fast-growing trees, enjoying a warmer climate, so grow better in southern England and mainland Europe. They will withstand air pollution and urban soil conditions.

MANAGEMENT. They are wind-firm and rarely drop branches. In many continental European cities, such as Paris, *Platanus* are pleached. When grown in parks and open spaces, they are allowed develop their own natural shape. Given the density of leaves on *Platanus*, it can cast severe shade and it can be difficult to establish vegetation beneath. In such situations, trees are often crown-lifted, i.e. tree surgeons remove lower branches.

PESTS AND DISEASES. Anthracnose of plane (*Apiognomonia veneta*) is a serious disease on *Platanus*, particularly in Southern Europe, where it occurs in 16 countries. The pathogen causes leaf necrosis and premature leaf fall (Tello *et al.*, 2005). Trees respond by developing epicormic growth, but they lose their ornamental value.

PARTICULAR PLANTING SCHEMES OR PLANT ASSOCIATIONS. An example of a formal planting is a 200-year-old avenue in the Sotos Históricos de Aranjuez, Spain (Fig. 4.8).
    Platanus × *hispanica* (London plane) is widely planted in London. Planted along the Thames on either side of the Houses of Parliament, their size and large numbers are in scale with the building, but their simplicity of green foliage in summer and tracery of branches in winter contrast with the ornate Victorian Gothic buildings (Fig. 4.9).

Fig. 4.8. 200-year-old avenue of *Platanus* in the Sotos Históricos de Aranjuez, Spain.

Fig. 4.9. *Platanus* × *hispanica* (London plane) by the Houses of Parliament, London.

P. orientalis is used as a street and amenity park tree in Greece and Turkey, where it is native.

Rhamnaceae *Rhamnus* and *Ceanothus*

These are shrubs cultivated for their evergreen foliage or for their flowers. Some species are native to Britain and Ireland. Few blue-flowering shrubs exist and this family includes one such genus, *Ceanothus*.

TYPES OF PLANTS. Shrubs: medium to large bushy shrubs.

WORLD DISTRIBUTION. California (*Ceanothus*) and Europe (*Rhamnus* and *Frangula*).

LEAVES. Foliage is deciduous or evergreen, alternate or opposite.

FLOWERS. Depending on genus, flowers are composed of four or five small sepals and petals.

FRUIT. Fruit is in the form of a drupe-like berry, red maturing to black (*Rhamnus*), or a dry capsule (*Ceanothus*).

GROWTH RATE AND LONGEVITY. They are fast-growing shrubs. *Ceanothus* tend to be short-lived and die out after 15–20 years.

FUNCTIONAL AND ORNAMENTAL USES.

Shrubberies	
Ground cover	Some cultivars of *Ceanothus*, e.g. *C. thyrsiflorus* var. *repens*
Blue flowers	*Ceanothus*
Native and naturalistic planting schemes	*Rhamnus cathartica* and *Frangula alnus*
Variegated shrub	*Rhamnus alaternus* 'Argenteovariegata'

GROWING CONDITIONS. They require dryish sites. *Ceanothus* thrive in milder sites with good drainage.

MANAGEMENT. *Ceanothus*: prune lightly after flowering. They do not respond to very severe pruning. *Rhamnus* can be pruned if they outgrow their allotted space and they will regrow.

PARTICULAR PLANTING SCHEMES OR PLANT ASSOCIATIONS. *Ceanothus* are very useful medium-sized to large shrubs for maritime areas and well-drained soils. Some are deciduous and others are evergreen. Leaf venation can be a useful tool for

Table 4.21. Sequence of flowering of commonly available *Ceanothus*.

Name	Time of flowering	Flower colour	Size of shrub Deciduous/evergreen
Ceanothus arboreus 'Trewithen Blue'	Late spring	Deep blue	Very large Evergreen
Ceanothus 'Southmead'	Early summer	Mid blue	Medium Evergreen
Ceanothus thyrsiflorus var. *repens*	Early summer	Mid blue	Ground cover Evergreen
Ceanothus 'Concha'	Early summer	Dark blue	Medium to large Evergreen
Ceanothus gloriosus 'Emily Brown'	Early summer	Dark blue	Ground cover Evergreen
Ceanothus 'Autumnal Blue'	Late summer and early autumn	Dark blue	Medium Evergreen
Ceanothus × *delileanus* 'Gloire de Versailles'	Late summer and early autumn	Pale blue	Medium Deciduous

identification of the genus when the shrubs are not in flower. Veins on the undersurface of the leaf are either pinnately veined or three-veined from the base of the leaf. Individually the flowers are tiny but the overall effect as they crowd into dense panicles is striking and showy. It is the only genus of blue-flowering shrubs grown out of doors in Western Europe. Depending on species or cultivar, they flower from late spring to early autumn. Spring-flowering species sometimes give a second flush of flower in the autumn (Table 4.21).

Rhamnus alaternus 'Argenteovariegata': leaves evergreen, alternate, a fast-growing, useful, dense, tall shrub. It is a useful shrub in urban landscape situations where other shrubs are difficult to establish.

Rhamnus cathartica (buckthorn) and *Frangula alnus* (alder buckthorn) are native in Britain and Ireland. Deciduous, they develop attractive golden autumn colours and are clothed in black fruit.

Members of other genera of the *Rhamnaceae*, such as *Paliuris* and *Colletia*, are confined to collections.

Rosaceae Rose

Members of this family make a major contribution to the range of trees and shrubs grown in landscape schemes and parks, as well as providing edible fruits for the table and for wildlife. They also make a major contribution to the range of native and introduced perennials in cultivation in Western Europe.

TYPES OF PLANTS. Trees: small to medium-sized trees – *Crataegus* (q.v.), *Malus* (q.v.), *Prunus* (q.v.), *Sorbus* (q.v.), *Pyrus* (q.v.) and distinguishing features of rosaceous trees commonly used in landscape schemes are given in Table 4.22.

Table 4.22. Distinguishing features of rosaceous trees commonly used in landscape schemes.

Features of genus	*Crataegus*	*Malus*	*Prunus*	*Pyrus*	*Sorbus*
Size (m)	To 15	To *c.*10	5–10–20	To 6–20	To 8–20
Shape	Dome-shaped, spreading	Dome-shaped, some upright	Various shapes	Tall, upright or small, pendulous tree	Various shapes
Leaf	Entire or lobe-leaved	Narrow leaves, some broad-leaved, many hairy-leaved beneath	Leaves narrow to elliptic with serrated edges and glands at the base of the blade	Shiny green or willow-leaved	Entire, some hairy beneath, or pinnate with 9–27 leaflets
Autumn colour			Spectacular in *Prunus serrulata*		Spectacular in *Sorbus sargentiana*
Time of flowering	May	April–May	Dec.–early June, depending on species	February	May–June
Colour of flower	White, red	White, pink and wine-red	White, pink	White	White
Stamens	5–25	15–50	Numerous	18–30	20
Style	2–5	2–5, united at base	1	2–5, free at base	2–5
Time of fruiting	Autumn–winter	Late summer–autumn	Mid-summer	Autumn	Autumn–winter
Fruit	Clusters of red haws	Tiny apple	Small plum or cherry	Small green pears	Clusters of orange, red or yellow berries
Other	Thorns on branches	Glands on leaf stalk	Thorns on branches (*Prunus spinosa*)		

Shrubs: small- to large-growing, easy to grow, reliable shrubs, widely available in the trade, e.g. *Chaenomeles, Cotoneaster* (q.v.), *Potentilla, Rosa* (q.v.) and *Rubus.*

WORLD DISTRIBUTION. *Rosaceae* are native to the northern temperate regions of the world.

LEAVES. Leaves are alternate, generally with a pair of stipules at the base of the leaf. Depending on the species, some are deciduous, others are evergreen and a few are semi-evergreen. Some are entire, as in *Malus,* and others pinnate, as in *Sorbus,* or palmately compound, as in *Potentilla.*

FLOWERS. Ornamental interest can be derived from the overall inflorescence, e.g. *Pyracantha* and *Prunus laurocerasus,* or from an individual flower, e.g.

Potentilla or *Chaenomeles* (quince). Flowers have four to five petals and four to five sepals, situated on top of a receptacle holding the ovaries. The predominant flower colour is white, with some species having pink, red or yellow flowers. Flowers are single. Double forms of *Rosa* (roses) and *Prunus* (cherry) have been developed by horticulturists over the centuries.

FRUIT. Many genera – *Malus, Prunus, Sorbus, Cotoneaster* and *Pyracantha* – develop ornamental fruit in late summer and autumn. Some fruits are held on the trees or shrubs throughout the winter months.

GROWTH RATE AND LONGEVITY. They are fast-growing plants. Trees live for approximately 50 years before they senesce.

FUNCTIONAL AND ORNAMENTAL USES.

Hedges and screens	*Prunus laurocerasus* and *Crataegus monogyna*
Street trees	e.g. *Sorbus* (rowan)
Motorway planting schemes	e.g. *Sorbus aucuparia*
Barrier planting schemes	*Rubus cockburnianus*
Shrubberies	e.g. *Prunus laurocerasus* and *P. lusitanica*
Ground-cover schemes	e.g. *Cotoneaster*
Naturalistic schemes	e.g. *Sorbus aucuparia*, and *S. aria, Prunus spinosa* (sloe)
Wildlife habitats	*S. aucuparia, C. monogyna, P. spinosa*
Food for birds in winter	e.g. *S. aria* and *S. aucuparia*
Flowering trees and shrubs	e.g. *Prunus* (cherry) and *Crataegus*
Fruiting trees	e.g. *Malus* (crab apple)
Autumn colour	e.g. *Prunus serrulata* and *Crataegus persimilis* 'Prunifolia'

GROWING CONDITIONS. They will grow in a variety of soils and situations. However, they should not be grown in soil where members of this family have already been cultivated. Among apple growers this condition is known as 'apple replant problem' or among rose growers as 'rose sickness'. On a limited scale soil can be replaced but on a large scale it is best to select species from other families.

MANAGEMENT. Trees require little pruning except for formative pruning in the early years and removal of senescent branches.

Shrubs can be pruned and they will withstand severe pruning if they become overgrown. Care must be taken with the time of pruning so that the succeeding season's flower or fruit will not be lost.

PESTS AND DISEASES. Of all the families described in this work, the family *Rosaceae* is most at risk from diseases. Peach leaf curl (*Taphrina deformans*), silver leaf (*Stereum*) and bacterial canker (*Pseudomonas syringae*) occur on trees in the genus *Prunus* and canker (*Nectria*) on *Malus* and *Pyrus*. Fireblight (*Erwinia amylovora*) can occur on all members of the family. Some local authorities prohibit the planting of certain genera. Black spot (*Diplocarpon rosae*) and aphids can be a problem on ornamental roses and a regular spray programme is necessary in rose gardens.

OTHER. In general, members of this family are widely available in the trade.

PARTICULAR PLANTING SCHEMES OR PLANT ASSOCIATIONS. In Britain and Ireland suburban streets lined with *Prunus* (cherry), *Crataegus* (hawthorn) and *Sorbus* (rowan) were and are common sights in cities.

In May and early June, thousands of miles of hedgerow in Britain and Ireland are white with the blossom of *Crataegus* (hawthorn, whitethorn or maybush).

The following are some reliable shrubs grown in shrubberies in parks and open spaces: *Chaenomeles, Exochorda, Kerria japonica, Photinia, Prunus laurocerasus, P. lusitanica, Pyracantha, Rhaphiolepis* and *Spiraea*.

The following ground-cover plants belong to the *Rosaceae*: *Chaenomeles japonica* (some cultivars), *Cotoneaster congestus, C. dammeri, C. horizontalis, C. microphyllus, C. salicifolius* 'Repens', *C. × suecicus* 'Skogholm', *Potentilla fruticosa, Rosa* 'Pauli', *R.* 'Nozomi', *R. rugosa* and cultivars, *Rubus rolfei, R. tricolor* and *Stephanandra incisa*.

Climbers: none other than among roses (q.v.).

The following hedging plants belong to the *Rosaceae*:

Deciduous species: *Crataegus monogyna* (hawthorn), *Prunus* 'Cistena' and *P. spinosa* (sloe).

Evergreen species: *Prunus laurocerasus* (cherry laurel) and *P. lusitanica* (Portuguese laurel).

Flowering species: *Cotoneaster lacteus, C. simonsii, Pyracantha* and *Rosa rugosa* and cultivars.

Crataegus (hawthorn)

TYPES OF PLANTS. Trees: small- to medium-sized trees with a broad-spreading habit.

WORLD DISTRIBUTION. North America, Europe, Western Asia and Japan.

LEAVES. Shoots have sharp thorns which vary in size depending on the species. Leaves lobed, with one to four lobes on each side of the leaf; or entire, with a toothed margin.

FLOWERS. Many-flowered inflorescences with white or pink flowers borne in May on bare wood.

FRUIT. Red or black haws are produced in September and, depending on the species, will last on the trees until February/March of the following year.

AUTUMN COLOUR. *Crataegus persimilis* 'Prunifolia' produces stunning autumn colour.

GROWTH RATE AND LONGEVITY. They are long-lived trees and were once commonly planted in urban parks and streets.

FUNCTIONAL AND ORNAMENTAL USES.

Native and naturalistic schemes	*Crataegus monogyna* and *C. laevigata*
Hedges in rural areas	*C. monogyna* and *C. laevigata*
Street trees	*C. laevigata* 'Paul's Scarlet'

GROWING CONDITIONS. They are fast-growing, easy to establish and will withstand difficult growing situations.

MANAGEMENT. Hedges are pruned on an annual basis. For trees, see Chapter 5, Trees: Selection, Use and Management.

PARTICULAR PLANTING SCHEMES OR PLANT ASSOCIATIONS. *Crataegus* (hawthorn) is the predominant hedge in rural areas in Britain and Ireland. In May, hedgerows are wreathed in white flowers, a spectacular sight.

Several *Crataegus* found in collections deserve to be more widely planted, e.g. *Crataegus orientalis*, a small tree with dainty foliage, is suitable for a small courtyard/patio garden.

C. laevigata 'Paul's Scarlet' is a long-lived street tree of medium size that will withstand poor growing conditions.

Malus (crab apple)

TYPES OF PLANTS. Trees: small- to medium-sized trees. Generally they are dome-shaped and wide-spreading (Fig. 2.1)

Shrubs: some *Malus* can be grown as shrubs, e.g. *Malus baccata*.

They are deciduous flowering trees, reliable in flower each year, and some species fruit prolifically. Selected varieties have become the culinary and dessert apples of commerce. A list of ornamental *Malus* generally available in the trade is given in Table 4.23.

Table 4.23. Common *Malus* crab apples available in the trade.

Malus floribunda
Malus 'Golden Hornet'
Malus × *schreideckeri* 'Hillieri'
Malus × *moerlandsii* 'Profusion'
Malus × *zumi* var. *calocarpa* 'John Downie'
Malus × *purpurea*
Malus 'Red Glow'
Malus 'Red Sentinal'
Malus 'Royalty'
Malus toringo
Malus tschonskii

WORLD DISTRIBUTION. A northern hemisphere genus native to North America, Japan, Siberia and China.

LEAVES. Narrow or rounded leaves are alternate, usually simple. They are usually glabrous above and some species or cultivars are downy beneath. Some trees with purple foliage – *Malus × purpurea* and its related cultivars – are available in the trade.

FLOWERS. Two to five styles united at the base distinguish *Malus* from *Prunus*, which has one style. There are five free petals, and flowers are generally white, pink or pinkish white.

FRUIT. Red, orange, yellow fruits, like miniature apples, which they are. Fruits vary in size and shape, being globose, round or conical. The calyx is persistent on some species and cultivars and not on others. The fruit might be sour and unpalatable but is not poisonous.

GROWTH RATE AND LONGEVITY. Trees establish quickly and flower and fruit when young. They will live for 40–50 years.

FUNCTIONAL AND ORNAMENTAL USES.

Street trees	*Malus × purpurea*
Park and amenity trees	*M. floribunda*
Garden trees	*M. × zumi* var. *calocarpa* 'John Downie'
Native/naturalistic planting schemes	*M. sylvestris*
Ornamental fruiting trees	*M. × zumi* var. *calocarpa* 'John Downie' and *M.* 'Golden Hornet'

GROWING CONDITIONS. They will grow in a variety of soils and situations. Where they are cultivated for their ornamental fruit, a number of individual trees should be grown together so that cross pollination can occur.

MANAGEMENT. Trees require little attention apart from regular checks of stakes and ties on recently planted trees.

PARTICULAR PLANTING SCHEMES OR PLANT ASSOCIATIONS. At Sutton Place, Guildford, Surrey, the 'Theatre Garden' is lined on three sides by *Malus × zumi* var. *calocarpa* 'John Downie'.

Prunus (cherry, plum, peach and almond)

TYPES OF PLANTS. Trees: small, medium and large trees.
    Shrubs: small- to large-growing shrubs.
    Flowering cherries are a well-known and popular group of trees with the general public. Depending on the species, they flower from winter to early

summer. They are freely available in the trade. Members of this genus are also important commercial fruit crops, in particular, cherries, peaches and nectarines.

WORLD DISTRIBUTION. A cosmopolitan genus, most species are native to the northern temperate regions. *Prunus avium* (gean) (Fig. 4.10) and *Prunus padus* (bird cherry) occur in the wild in Britain and Ireland.

LEAVES. Foliage is deciduous or evergreen, alternate, glabrous, varying in size from 10 to 20 cm.

FLOWERS. Five petals, five sepals and one style distinguish *Prunus* from *Malus*, which has two to five styles. Depending on the botanical section of the genus, flowers are stalked or stalkless, solitary, in clusters or in racemes. Flowers are white or pink, single or double. Depending on the species, flowers are borne from November to late June (Table 4.24). In *P. padus* (bird cherry) and its allies, flowers are in racemes.

FRUIT. A single stone at the centre of the fruit surrounded by a fleshy drupe distinguishes *Prunus* from *Malus*. Fruit is variously coloured: red (*P. avium*), purple or amber (*P. cerasifera*), purple (*P. spinosa* (sloe)). Fruit in *P. padus* and in the evergreen species is black. Fruit is borne from mid- to late summer. Unlike other members of the *Rosaceae* family, this genus is not grown ornamentally for its fruit, though in well-favoured areas fruiting may occur.

AUTUMN COLOUR. Some *Prunus serrulata* cultivars and *P. sargentii* develop spectacular autumn colour.

Fig. 4.10. *Prunus avium*, gean, with flowers and fruit. (From Savill, 1991.)

Table 4.24. Sequence of flowering of *Prunus* from November–June.

Name	Common name	Shape	Flower colour
Prunus x *subhirtella* 'Autumnalis'	Winter-flowering cherry	Dome-shaped	Pink
Prunus dulcis	Almond	Spreading	Pink
Prunus cerasifera 'Nigra'	Purple plum	Dome-shaped	Pink
Prunus pendula 'Pendula Rosea'		Distinctly dome-shaped	Pink
Prunus triloba 'Multiplex'		Small tree with long shoots studded with double flowers	Pink
Prunus serrula		V-shaped	Pink, mahogany-coloured bark
Prunus × *yedoensis*	Yoshino cherry	Broad-spreading	Pink
Prunus 'Okame'		V-shaped	Pink
Prunus × *subhirtella* 'Fukubana'		Broad-spreading	Pink
Prunus maackii	Manchurian cherry	Upswept branches	White, amber-coloured bark
Prunus spinosa	Sloe	Bushy, small tree	White
Prunus avium	Gean	Upswept branches	White
Prunus serrulata		Various shapes	Pink/white
Prunus 'Amanogawa'		Columnar	Pink
Prunus 'Kanzan'		Vase-shaped	Pink
Prunus 'Tai Haku'		Horizontal	White
Prunus 'Shirotae'		Horizontal	White
Prunus 'Ukon'		Vase-shaped	Green
Prunus padus	Bird cherry	Upswept branches	White
Prunus laurocerasus and cultivars	Cherry laurel	Shrub	White
Prunus lusitanica	Portuguese laurel	Shrub	White

BARK. *Prunus serrula* and *P. maackii* have mahogany-brown-coloured bark and amber-coloured bark, respectively (Fig. 2.18). Branches with bands of lenticels distinguish *Prunus* from other genera.

GROWTH RATE AND LONGEVITY. Fast-growing plants, easy to establish. Trees from this genus live for about 50 years.

FUNCTIONAL AND ORNAMENTAL USES.

Hedges and screens	*Prunus lusitanica* and *P. laurocerasus*
Street trees and amenity trees	e.g. *Prunus* 'Pandora' and *P. padus* (Fig. 4.11)
Shade and poor soil conditions	*P. laurocerasus* and *P. lusitanica*
Ground cover	*P. laurocerasus* 'Zabelliana' and *P. laucerasus l.* 'Otto Luyken'

GROWING CONDITIONS. They will grow in a variety of soils and situations. In windswept sites *P. serrulata* can become lopsided and shaped by the direction of the prevailing wind.

Fig. 4.11. A line of *Prunus padus* on a suburban road in Dublin.

MANAGEMENT. Evergreen species of *Prunus* will withstand severe pruning and will regenerate successfully.

P. laurocerasus has become naturalized in many woodland estates, where it can be labour-intensive and difficult to eradicate.

P. serrulata have surface roots and where space is limited they will lift pavements and kerbs, causing hazards to members of the public. Some municipal authorities have begun to remove these trees from street tree planting schemes.

Some *P. serrulata* are grafted on to *Prunus domestica* and where the stock sprouts from the base of the tree it should be removed.

PESTS AND DISEASES. Bacterial canker (*Pseudomonas syringae*), causing circular brown patches in the leaf, occurs in *Prunus*. The severity of damage to leaves can vary from season to season.

Peach leaf curl (*Taphrina deformans*), a fungus, causes contorted, reddened foliage to develop on peaches and almonds.

PARTICULAR PLANTING SCHEMES OR PLANT ASSOCIATIONS. *Prunus serrulata* (Japanese cherry) and *P. cerasifera* 'Pissardii' (purple-leaved plum) are commonly planted trees in suburban gardens in Dublin.

Prunus × hillieri 'Spire' is grown as a street tree in Germany.

At Powerscourt, County Wicklow, Ireland, and Mount Stewart, County Down, Northern Ireland, large, clipped, dome-shaped *P. lusitanica* accentuate the formality of the walled garden and Italian garden, respectively.

Pyrus (pear)

TYPES OF PLANTS. Trees: *Pyrus* are small- to medium-sized trees with a narrow upright growth habit or with pendulous bushy growth and grey foliage.

WORLD DISTRIBUTION. Europe, Western Asia and China.

LEAVES. Unlike other tree genera of the *Rosaceae*, foliage is shiny green, ovate to elliptic in outline. Autumn colour is poor and foliage is held on the tree late into the autumn. In one species, *Pyrus salicifolia* 'Pendula', foliage is grey in colour and long and narrow, like that of *Salix* (willow).

FLOWERS. White flowers 2–4 cm are held in clusters on bare wood in February–March.

FRUIT. Small pear-shaped fruit occurs on *P. salicifolia* 'Pendula'.

GROWTH RATE AND LONGEVITY. Trees will establish easily and grow for some 40–60 years.

FUNCTIONAL AND ORNAMENTAL USES
Street tree	*Pyrus calleryana* 'Chanticleer' and *P. communis* 'Beech Hill'
Ornamental weeping tree	*P. salicifolia* 'Pendula'
Grey-foliaged tree	*P. salicifolia* 'Pendula'

GROWING CONDITIONS. They are suited to many soils and situations. They are tolerant of drought and moisture.

MANAGEMENT. *Pyrus calleryana* 'Chanticleer' was commonly planted as a street tree. It has an upright growth habit with narrowly spaced branches. As the tree matures it can 'split apart' and falling branches could cause damage to people and vehicles.

PARTICULAR PLANTING SCHEMES OR PLANT ASSOCIATIONS. A well-rounded specimen of *P. salicifolia* 'Pendula' forms the centrepiece of the White Garden at Sissinghurst, Kent, England.

Sorbus (rowan or mountain ash, whitebeam)

TYPES OF PLANTS. Trees: small- to medium-sized trees 8–15–20 m.
Generally they are densely branched, with upswept branches creating a rounded or ovoid outline.
Shrubs: there are a number of shrubby species which are confined to collections. *Sorbus reducta*, a diminutive, suckering shrub, is not in general landscape use but would be a suitable under-shrub in courtyards and confined spaces.

WORLD DISTRIBUTION. A cosmopolitan genus of deciduous species, from the northern hemisphere, China, Himalaya, Europe and eastern North America. Some species are native to Europe, e.g. *Sorbus aria, S. aucuparia* and *S. torminalis* (Fig. 4.12).

LEAVES. Leaves are alternate. Based on their leaves, *Sorbus* are divided into two main groups, the Aria section, with entire leaves and noticeable veins on the undersurface of the leaves, and the Aucuparia section, with pinnate leaves,

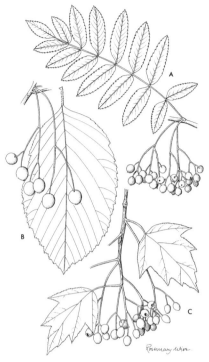

Fig. 4.12. Variation in leaf among *Sorbus*: (A) *Sorbus aucuparia*, rowan; (B) *Sorbus aria*, whitebeam; (C) *Sorbus torminalis*, wild service tree. (From Savill, 1991.)

varying from 11–25 leaflets. Leaves unfold in May or June about the same time as the flowers blossom.

FLOWERS. Inflorescence is corymbose, 6–10 cm broad. Each flower has five petals, which are generally white or pinkish white, and 15–20 stamens.

FRUIT. Red, orange, brown, white or yellow fruit is borne in autumn in clusters of globose fruit. They are often held long after the leaves have fallen. While birds feed on the red-fruited *Sorbus*, they are less inclined to take other coloured fruits. Fruit colour of common and less common *Sorbus* trees is given in Table 4.25.

AUTUMN COLOUR. Particularly good in *Sorbus sargentiana* and *S.* 'Joseph Rock'.

BARK. Mature specimens of *Sorbus* 'Joseph Rock' develop a pale plum-hued bark.

GROWTH RATE AND LONGEVITY. *Sorbus* are fast-growing and live for 40–60 years.

FUNCTIONAL AND ORNAMENTAL USES.

Street trees	*S. aucuparia* 'Shearwater Seedling' and *S. thuringiaca* 'Fastigiata' (Fig. 2.5).
Public parks	*S. intermedia* and *S.* 'Joseph Rock'
Naturalistic schemes, wildlife habitats and motorway planting schemes	*S. aucuparia* and *S. aria*

GROWING CONDITIONS. They will grow in a variety of soils and situations. The Chinese species prefer good soil and an open position and are sensitive to heat and drought. They are cultivated in Northern rather than Southern Europe.

MANAGEMENT. The soil around the trees should be kept weed-free. As trees develop, some formative pruning may be necessary. Some *Sorbus* are grafted on to *S. aucuparia* or *Crataegus* rootstock and where the stock sprouts from the base of the tree it should be removed.

PARTICULAR PLANTING SCHEMES OR PLANT ASSOCIATIONS. *S. aria* 'Lutescens' is a common landscape tree; the unfolding foliage is clothed in white hairs and

Table 4.25. Fruit colour of common and less common *Sorbus* trees.

Name	Fruit colour	Foliage type
Sorbus aria	Red	Simple
Sorbus aucuparia	Red	Pinnate
Sorbus aucuparia 'Sheerwater Seedling'	Red	Pinnate
Sorbus cashmiriana	White	Pinnate
Sorbus hupehensis	Whitish pink	Pinnate
Sorbus intermedia	Orange/red	Partly lobed
Sorbus 'Joseph Rock'	Yellow	Pinnate
Sorbus sargentiana	Red	Pinnate
Sorbus scalaris	Red	Pinnate
Sorbus × *thuringiaca* 'Fastigiata'	Red	Partly lobed
Sorbus torminalis	Brown	Lobed similar to *Acer*
Sorbus vilmorinii	Pinkish white	Pinnate

sits like a white candle on the branches of the tree. *S. aria* and *S. aria* 'Magnifica' are commonly cultivated as street trees in Germany.

S. aucuparia 'Sheerwater Seedling' and *S.* × *thuringiaca* 'Fastigiata', with their lollypop shape, are common landscape trees in business parks and in streets where space is limited.

At Castlewellan, County Down, Northern Ireland, a double row of *Sorbus hupehensis* form a canopy over a flight of steps leading from one section of the arboretum to another.

In Durham, England, two *S. intermedia* planted together read as one tree and create a distinctive feature in a small public park.

At the Glebe Gallery, County Donegal, Ireland, the artist Derek Hill, planting with a painter's eye, surrounded a single specimen of *Sorbus hedlundii* (with broad elliptic leaves) with a semicircle of *Betula pendula* (with small triangular-shaped leaves).

Shrubby genera in the *Rosaceae*

Cotoneaster

TYPES OF PLANTS. Trees: a shrubby tree attaining tree-like proportions, small- to medium-sized trees, e.g. *Cotoneaster frigidus*.

Shrubs: small- to large-growing shrubs freely available in the trade. Many are attractive in habit, and their habit, mat-forming, ground-hugging or serpentine-branching, leads to their use as ground cover and shrubbery plants.

Major species of *Cotoneaster* in cultivation and their uses are given in Table 4.26.

WORLD DISTRIBUTION. Native to China and Himalaya.

LEAVES. Foliage is alternate, simple, deciduous semi-evergreen or evergreen. Leaves vary in size from very tiny (*Cotoneaster microphyllus*) to large

Table 4.26. Main species of *Cotoneaster* in cultivation and their uses.

Name	Habit	Function and size (m)
Cotoneaster congestus	Flat, ground-hugging	Ground cover
Cotoneaster dammeri	Flat, ground-hugging	Ground cover
Cotoneaster frigidus 'Cornubia'	Upswept arching branches	Large shrub 8–10
Cotoneaster horizontalis	Herringbone pattern	Ground cover
Cotoneaster 'Hydridus Pendulus'	Small tree with pendulous habit	Small ornamental tree, 3–4
Cotoneaster lacteus	Upswept arching branches	Large hedge or tree, 3–4
Cotoneaster microphyllus	Stiff spreading branches	Ground cover
Cotoneaster salicifolius	Upright	Large shrub, 3–4
Cotoneaster salicifolius 'Repens'	Flat with arching stems	Ground cover
Cotoneaster simonsii	Stiff upright stems	Hedge, 1–2
Cotoneaster × *suecicus* 'Coral Beauty'	Flat with arching stems	Ground cover
Cotoneaster × *suecicus* 'Skogholm'	Bushy	Ground cover
Cotoneaster × *watereri*	Broad head	Large shrub, 7

(6–12 cm) (*C. lacteus* and *C. salicifolius*). Leaves vary from glabrous to hairy to thickly felted with a suede-like, dense, hairy covering beneath.

FLOWERS. Borne April–June, with five free petals, flowers are generally white to pinkish white. Some are single and others are in clusters. Some are showy and conspicuous in flower, e.g. *C. frigidus*, others are not, e.g. *C. simonsii*.

FRUIT. Their most attractive feature, fruit colour, varies from light to deep red, with some black- and a few yellow-fruited species and cultivars. Fruit is held singly, e.g. *C. microphyllus*, or in clusters of tiny fruit, e.g. *C. lacteus*. Each fruit has three to five nutlets.

GROWTH RATE AND LONGEVITY. They are fast-growing shrubs and will live for many years.

FUNCTIONAL AND ORNAMENTAL USES. *Cotoneaster* is used to form hedges and screens, shrubberies, ground cover schemes, naturalistic schemes and wildlife habitats. They are useful on embankments, slopes and rock outcrops.

GROWING CONDITIONS. They grow in all but the poorest soils.

MANAGEMENT. They can be pruned and will regenerate satisfactorily.

PESTS AND DISEASES. *C. salicifolius* is particularly susceptible to fireblight *Erwinia amylovora*.

PARTICULAR PLANTING SCHEMES OR PLANT ASSOCIATIONS. *Cotoneaster lucidus*, a Siberian species, is a common landscape shrub in Oslo, Norway.

Fine hedges of *C. lacteus* rival those of *Ilex aquifolium*, *Fagus sylvatica* and *Carpinus betulus* in stature and majesty.

Several *Cotoneaster* are cultivated as standards by the nursery trade. They form small standard trees suitable for gardens or small courtyards, e.g. *C.* 'Hybridus Pendulus', *C.* 'Coral Beauty' and *C. congestus*.

Rosa (rose)

TYPES OF PLANTS. Shrubs: small- to large-growing shrubs, widely available in the trade.

Climbers: many species are vigorous climbers but they are little used in landscape work. However, hybrid rambling and climbing roses have been bred and they are grown on walls and trellises.

A genus of great importance in all aspects of horticulture, both floriculture and amenity use. They have long been in cultivation in both the East and the West and from earliest times forms of species roses have been selected for use not only for garden ornament but for perfumery. Breeding of roses has led to many groups of cultivated roses, commonly referred to as shrub roses. In the late 19th century, breeders developed hybrid tea roses (or large-flowered roses) and in the 20th century, floribunda (cluster roses), which were to become the popular garden rose of millions of private gardeners. In recent years, roses for low-maintenance landscape schemes have been bred and are available in the nursery trade. Categories of roses in cultivation are listed in Table 4.27.

WORLD DISTRIBUTION. Native to the northern hemisphere, roses occur in western China, central Asia, Europe, Britain and Ireland.

LEAVES. Foliage is deciduous, alternate, odd pinnate, with a varying number of leaflets. Foliage is matt in the species roses, and glossy, often emerging red and then becoming green, in the hybrid tea and floribunda roses.

FLOWERS. Species roses have five free petals with numerous stamens. Cultivated roses have single, semi-double and double flowers. All colours except blue are represented in the flowers. Depending on the species or cultivar, they flower from May until early winter. Species roses flower once, while cultivated roses can produce one or more flushes of flowers per year.

FRUIT. Hips (or heps) are red or orange-coloured and round or oval to flagon-shaped.

GROWTH RATE AND LONGEVITY. They are fast-growing and easy to establish. Roses will live for 20–30 years.

Table 4.27. Categories of roses in cultivation.

Types of roses	Example	
Species roses	*Rosa filipes*	'Kiftsgate'
	Rosa helenae	
	Rosa moyesii	
	Rosa rugosa	'Alba', 'Blanc Double de Coubert', 'Frau Dagmar Hastrup', 'Roseraie de l'Haÿ'
Types of shrub roses		
Damask	'Célina'	
Dwarf polyantha	'Perle d'Or'	
Gallica	*gallica* 'Versicolor'	
	'Tuscany'	
Hybrid perpetual	'Ferdinard Picard'	
Moss	'William Lobb'	
Modern roses		
Climbers	'Maigold'	
	'Sunday Times'	
English roses	'Constance Spry'	
Floribunda	'Elizabeth of Glamis'	
	'Iceberg'	
Hybrid tea	'Peace'	
	'Whisky Mac'	
Ramblers	'Rambling Rector'	
	'American Pillar'	
Landscape roses		
Ground cover	'Nozomi'	
	County Park series named for English counties, e.g. 'Essex', and a series named for birds, e.g. 'Grouse', 'Partridge', 'Pheasant'	

FUNCTIONAL AND ORNAMENTAL USES

Rose gardens	Some fine examples include St Annes, Raheny, Dublin; Sir Thomas and Lady Dixon Park, Belfast; Hyde Park and Syon House, London; Castle Howard, Yorkshire; and Garden of the Rose, St Albans.
Hedges and screens	e.g. *R.* 'Perle d'Or', *R. rugosa*
Ground-cover shrubs	e.g. *R.* 'Nozomi'
Scented shrubs	e.g. *R.* 'Ena Harkness', *R. rugosa* 'Roseraie de l'Hay'
Autumn colour	Some of the species roses, e.g. *R. moyesii* and *R. rugosa* and its hybrids, develop attractive autumn colour

GROWING CONDITIONS. They will grow in a variety of soils and situations.

MANAGEMENT. An annual pruning regime is required for hybrid tea and floribunda roses.

Many hybrid tea and floribunda roses are grafted and any stock that develops can be removed. In a landscape situation where shrubs such as *R. rugosa* are grown, they should be grown on their own roots; removing suckers from such situations is troublesome and time-consuming.

Modern roses developed for use in hedges and ground-cover schemes require little or no pruning and would be treated as any other hedge or ground-cover scheme.

PESTS AND DISEASES. Where a large number of roses are grown, aphids and black spot can occur and regular spraying is necessary.

PARTICULAR PLANTING SCHEMES OR PLANT ASSOCIATIONS. Ground-cover roses mark the approach to Broughshane near Ballymena, County Antrim, Northern Ireland.

Rosa rugosa is grown to create an informal barrier planting between a path and road in suburban Bergen, Norway. It grows on sandhills near Copenhagen and in coastal gardens in the west of Ireland. It also creates an attractive ground cover on a sloping site in a car park in an industrial site in County Wicklow, Ireland.

Rosa canina (dog rose) and *R. spinosissima* (burnet rose) are native in Britain and Ireland. The former occurs in hedgerows, the latter on sand dunes.

Shrub roses are grown in summer gardens, in association with other shrubs; good examples occur in the Harris Garden, University of Reading, and in Sissinghurst, Kent, England.

Other genera

As well as the genera *Cotoneaster* and *Rosa* described above, many other shrubby genera within the *Rosaceae* are important plants for landscape schemes. They are briefly described in Table 4.28 and their use and management are discussed below.

SPRING-FLOWERING SHRUBS. *Chaenomeles japonica* (quince) is an early spring-flowering shrub, flowering on bare stems. The fruit, which is like a misshapen lemon, is borne in the autumn and held over the winter months. It is cultivated as a wall shrub and as a free-standing shrub. They can be pruned severely and will regenerate. There are many cultivars, in shades of red, pink and white flowers, examples being *Chaenomeles* × *superba* 'Rowallane', double red, *C.* × *superba* 'Pink Lady', pink, and *C. speciosa* 'Nivalis' white.

FLOWERING SHRUBS WITH SHOWY FLOWERS. *Kerria japonica* and *K. japonica* 'Pleniflora' are deciduous with yellow flowers borne on year-old wood in spring. After flowering, the shrub sends up new shoots not unlike those of bamboo, which bear flowers the following spring. Once the blossoms fade, flowering stems should be removed.

Table 4.28. Shrubby genera from the *Rosaceae* cultivated in landscape schemes.

Name	D	E	Habit	Function	Flower	Time of flowering	Fruit/ other features
Chaenomeles	x		Spreading or upright	Shrub, wall shrub	White, pink, red	Spring	Lemon-shaped
Eriobotrya		x	Upright	Specimen shrub for a wall			Like small yellow apples
Exochorda	x		Arching	Shrub	White	Early summer	
Kerria	x		Bamboo-like	Shrub	Yellow	Spring	
Photinia		x	Bushy shrub	Large shrub	White	Early summer	Young shoots red
Physocarpus	x		Bushy shrub	Large shrub	White	Summer	Purple foliage
Potentilla	x		Low-growing	Ground cover	White, yellow, pink, orange	Summer	
Pyracantha	x		Bushy shrub	Wall shrub, large shrub, hedge	White	Spring	Yellow, orange, red
Rhaphiolepis		x	Dome-shaped shrub	Small shrub	White	Early summer	
Rubus	x	x	Low-growing, arching	Ground cover, impenetrable shrubs	White	Summer	Occasional yellow raspberry
Sorbaria	x		Arching shrub		White	Mid-summer	
Spiraea	x	x	Low-growing and bushy shrub	Ground cover, shrub	White, deep pink	Early summer, autumn	
Stephanandra	x		Ground-hugging, upright stems	Ground cover, shrubs	Whitish	Mid-summer	Brown stems in winter

D, deciduous foliage; E, evergreen foliage.

Exochorda × *macrantha* 'The Bride' and *Spiraea* 'Arguta' are deciduous shrubs flowering in May. They are useful early-summer-flowering shrubs, part of the 'white cycle' of flowering shrubs in the period of late spring and summer. They have little to recommend them when not in flower but are useful shrubs for a range of situations in parks and open spaces. They are amenable to pruning.

Potentilla is a small semi-evergreen shrub suited to dry situations. It is native to North America, Europe and Asia. In Ireland it is one of the features of the flat limestone pavement at the Burren, County Clare. In the wild, flowers are yellow, but many cultivars in shades of yellow, tangerine, white and pink have been selected. A national collection of *Potentilla* is cultivated in Ardgillan Demesne, County Dublin (Halpenny and Simms, 2005).

Physocarpos opulifolius 'Diabolo' is a medium-sized, deciduous, purple-leaved plant with white flowers. It has become popular in recent years and it retains its strong purple colour through the season.

Sorbaria kirolowii is a mid-summer, off-white flowering shrub. The genus name suggests a similarity to *Sorbus;* it has pinnate leaves. It is large and deciduous, attractive for 'wilder', less manicured areas. The panicles of white flowers demonstrate its relationship to the herbaceous plants *Filipendula, Aruncus dioicus* and *Astilbe.* It has attractive brown stems in winter.

EVERGREEN SHRUBS. *Eriobotrya japonica* has bold dramatic foliage, not unlike that of a large-leaved *Rhododendron.* It is an excellent architectural shrub, even if it never flowers or fruits. It requires wall protection. *Rhaphiolepis umbellatus* forms a low hummock-shaped shrub for a sheltered site. White flowers, borne in June, are succeeded by small black fruits.

Photinia serratifolia and *P.* × *fraseri* 'Red Robin' are large-growing shrubs with glossy green leaves. Young shoots emerge red, in early summer, an attractive addition to a planting scheme. In the south of England it flowers well each summer, but in Ireland it seldom flowers in any profusion.

TOUGH, EASILY CULTIVATED SHRUBS. The genus *Rubus* (blackberry/bramble) provides a number of ground-cover species and some shrubs for difficult growing conditions. *Rubus tricolor* and *R. rolfei* have entire leaves and are armed with soft spines. They are widely used ground-cover species. *Rubus cockburnianus,* with pinnate foliage, is armed with large thorns and is useful when an impenetrable tangled mass of growth is required. It has attractive white stems in winter.

FRUITS. *Pyracantha* (firethorn) is an evergreen thorny shrub grown for its fruit in shades of orange, red and yellow. Trained against a wall it can attain 6–7 m and it is also grown as a large free-standing shrub. The following provide richly berried shrubs each year*: Pyracantha rogersiana, P. rogersiana* 'Flava' and *P.* 'Orange Glow'.

Rutaceae Rue

This family contains the citrus fruits, orange, lemon and grapefruit, some of which are cultivated as ornamentals in Mediterranean countries and as conservatory plants further north in Europe. Two genera, *Skimmia* and *Choisya,* are widely grown as landscape shrubs, while *Ruta* (rue) is cultivated in herb gardens.

TYPES OF PLANTS. Trees: e.g. *Phellodendron* and *Ptelea,* which are confined to collections.

Shrubs: small- to medium-sized shrubs.

WORLD DISTRIBUTION. Southern Europe, Mexico, New Zealand, Tasmania and Japan.

LEAVES. Foliage is evergreen or deciduous, opposite or alternate. The leaf shape is as follows: narrow elliptic in *Skimmia*; fern-like in *Ruta*; and trifoliate in *Choisya*. Foliage is scented when crushed.

FLOWERS. Various flower shapes occur: terminal panicle (*Skimmia*), terminal corymb (*Ruta*) and axillary corymb (*Choisya*). Each flower has four petals in *Ruta* and *Skimmia* and five petals in *Choisya*. In all flowers, many thick stamens surround a prominent ovary. In *Choisya* the white flowers are noticeably scented, giving the common name Mexican orange blossom. Flowers are yellow in *Ruta* and white in *Skimmia*. Like *Ilex* (holly), *Skimmia* is one of the few commonly cultivated genera where male and female occur on separate plants.

FRUIT. Red fruits looking superficially like *Ilex* (holly) berries occur in *Skimmia*. However, they are paler red and hollow inside and are of no value as food for birds.

GROWTH RATE AND LONGEVITY. *Skimmia* and *Ruta* are slow-growing, while *Choisya* is fast-growing. They are long-lived, sturdy shrubs.

FUNCTIONAL AND ORNAMENTAL USES.

Shrubberies	*Choisya ternata, Skimmia japonica*
Herb garden	*Ruta graveolens*
Grey foliage	*R. graveolens*
Industrial sites	*S. japonica*

GROWING CONDITIONS. *Skimmia* grows well in a moist, shaded area. Leaves become bleached in direct sunlight. *Choisya* thrives in a milder climate and can be damaged by cold winds in winter.

MANAGEMENT. In time *Choisya*, when planted in blocks or drifts, will form large dome-shaped shrubberies, which can 'break open'. In such situations plants can be severely pruned to within 0.5 m of ground level and they will regenerate.

Where *Skimmia* is grown for its berries, male and female plants should be planted.

PARTICULAR PLANTING SCHEMES OR PLANT ASSOCIATIONS. In University College Dublin and The Square shopping centre in Tallaght, Dublin, *Choisya ternata* is one of a range of landscape shrubs cultivated in large numbers.

In recent years two cultivars, *C. ternata* 'Sundance' with yellow foliage and *Choisya* 'Aztec Pearl' with dainty cut-leaved foliage, have become popular garden plants and are widely available in garden centres.

In *S. japonica* subsp. *reevesiana*, a male cultivar, 'Rubella', is particularly attractive in winter, when the developing inflorescence is deep red.

LESSER KNOWN GENERA. *Acradenia frankliniae*, with trifoliate, dark green, leathery leaves and dainty white flowers, borne in panicles in early summer, has a neat architectural habit for a sheltered site.

Correa 'Mannii', with a spreading habit, and *C. backhousiana*, with an upright habit, are evergreen shrubs with opposite green leaves. Tubular bell-shaped flowers in shades of pink and yellow are borne intermittently over the winter months. *Correa* is becoming more widely available in nurseries.

—————————— • ——————————

Salicaceae Poplar and Willow

Fast-growing trees suitable for damp sites. Several *Salix* and *Populus* are distinctive for their shape and habit (Figs. 2.7 and 2.8). Some species of *Salix* are grown for their fluffy catkins and are known as pussy willow.

TYPES OF PLANTS. Trees: small to medium to large.
     Shrubs: small to medium to large.

WORLD DISTRIBUTION. Europe, China and western North America.

LEAVES. Foliage is deciduous with alternate, entire leaves. In shape, foliage is often lanceolate in *Salix* (willow) and ovate or diamond-shaped in *Populus* (poplar) (Fig. 4.13). Foliage is matt green in *Salix* and shiny green in many *Populus*. *Populus tremula* is known for its incessant leaf quiver.

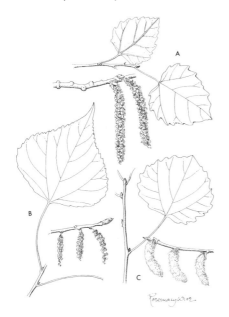

BUDS AND SHOOTS. In *Populus* the leaf bud is ovoid or narrow and lies parallel to the shoot. In *Salix* buds are very small, ovoid in shape. In both genera young shoots are coloured green, yellow, golden or orange.

FLOWERS. Male and female flowers occur on separate trees. They develop before the leaves and are conspicuous and ornamental. In *Populus* the male catkins, usually red, can be 4–8 cm in length. Female catkins are shorter (Fig. 4.13). In *Salix* male flowers are cylindrical, emerging in March and April. Female flowers are similar. They are often referred to as pussy willow.

FRUIT. Catkins of *Populus* develop into fluffy seeds (like small cotton buds) and are shed in June. Female catkins of *Salix* develop into fluffy fruits as the seeds mature, and they fall to the ground in late June.

Fig. 4.13. (A) *Populus* × *canescens*, grey poplar; (B) *Populus nigra* subsp. *betulifolia*, black poplar; (C) *Populus tremula*, aspen. (From Savill, 1991.)

GROWTH RATE AND LONGEVITY. Both genera are fast-growing, generally short-lived trees and shrubs.

FUNCTIONAL AND ORNAMENTAL USES.

Shelter belts	*Populus nigra* 'Italica'
Native and naturalistic planting schemes	*Salix* spp. and *P. tremula*
Soil stabilization	*Salix*

GROWING CONDITIONS. *Salix* (willow) grow in damp conditions.

MANAGEMENT. *Salix* and *Populus* are often cultivated from cuttings, which are planted directly into ground. They can be difficult to eradicate and are no longer commonly planted in motorway landscape schemes. They can be pruned severely.

PESTS AND DISEASES. *Salix* is prone to browning of foliage in summer.

PARTICULAR PLANTING SCHEMES OR PLANT ASSOCIATIONS. In the 1980s *Populus* and *Salix* were planted in Warrington and Runcorn, near Liverpool, where they were used to create fast-growing urban woodland.

Populus italica 'Nigra' (Lombardy poplar) is often seen as shelter belts in industrial estates.

Populus and × *Cupressocyparis* are grown to create a partly evergreen shelter belt (Figure 4.14).

Fig. 4.14. Shelter belt of *Populus* and × *Cupressocyparis leylandii.*

Populus × *jackii* 'Aurora' is an example of a tree that became popular with the gardening public. In the 1980s and 1990s it was widely planted as a garden tree and many remain.

Populus lasiocarpa (Chinese necklace poplar) is a majestic parkland tree, with, as the common name indicates, pendulous seed like black necklaces. It is limited to collections but deserves to be more widely planted.

Salix alba (tall green-leaved trees) interplanted with white-leaved *S. alba* 'Sericea' formed an effective screen on a busy road, the mixed planting being unobtrusive to drivers.

S. alba var. *vitellina* 'Britzensis' is the most common weeping tree by a pool or pond in a public garden. In England it is often seen on village greens.

Salix caprea is very common in the west of Ireland, where it occurs in field boundaries and by road margins. *S. caprea* 'Kilmarnock' a willow with a very distinct pendulous habit, and *S. matsudana* 'Tortuosa', with contorted branches, are often grown in suburban gardens.

Salix fargesii, a shrubby willow, is little used and undeservedly so. It is attractive in winter months because of its red stems and large buds and for its large, distinctly veined leaves in summer.

Salix hastata 'Wehrhahnii' is a slow-growing, hummock-shaped shrub with grey foliage, suitable for the edge of a shrubbery in a damp site.

———————————————— • ————————————————

Saxifragaceae

Depending on the book one reads, the genera described here, *Hydrangea*, *Deutzia*, *Philadelphus* (mock orange), *Ribes* (flowering currants) and *Escallonia*, are classified in various families or in the *Saxifragaceae*. They are all very useful genera, providing many flowering shrubs for landscape situations. All but one, *Escallonia*, are tough and hardy. The genus *Ribes* includes the bush fruits blackcurrant and gooseberry. Within the flower, the bifid stigma is a useful clue to the identification of the family.

TYPES OF PLANTS. Shrubs: small to large.
     Climber: to several metres.

WORLD DISTRIBUTION. China, Japan, Europe and Chile.

LEAVES. Foliage is deciduous and evergreen, alternate and entire.

FLOWERS. Clusters of flowers in racemes, panicles, cymes or corymbs. Flower shape varies with the genus (Table 4.29).

FRUIT. In *Ribes*, the fruit is a berry. In the other genera, it is a woody capsule with little ornamental value.

Table 4.29. Identification of genera in *Saxifragaceae* cultivated in landscape schemes.

Genus	Size (m)	Foliage	Flower colour	Flower shape	Time of flower
Deutzia	1–2	Deciduous, foliage opposite with stellate hairs, especially on undersurface of leaf	Pink	Clusters of flowers, each with 5 petals and 10 stamens, 5 tall and 5 short	Summer
Escallonia	1–3	Evergreen, glossy green, often scented	Pink, red, white	Clusters of tubular flowers	Summer
Hydrangea	1–2	Deciduous and evergreen	Blue, pink, mauve, white	Panicles or corymbs of flowers with 4 or 5 petals. Many also have sterile flowers at the margins of the inflorescence	Summer and autumn
Philadelphus	2–3	Deciduous, glabrous elliptic leaves	White, sometimes with a purple blotch	Clusters of scented flowers, each with 4 petals	Summer
Ribes	1–2	Deciduous, lobed or entire leaves	Yellow, red, pink	Many-flowered raceme	Spring

GROWTH RATE AND LONGEVITY. They are fast-growing, long-lived shrubs.

FUNCTIONAL AND ORNAMENTAL USES.

Summer-flowering shrubs	*Escallonia, Hydrangea* (most), *Philadelphus, Deutzia*
Spring-flowering shrubs	*Ribes*
Climbers	*Hydrangea anomala* var. *petiolaris*
Hedges	*Escallonia*

GROWING CONDITIONS. With the exception of *Escallonia* these genera can be cultivated in a range of landscape sites in urban areas. *Escallonia* is suited to maritime areas, where it can withstand salt spray.

MANAGEMENT. They can be pruned and will regenerate quickly.

GENERA from the *Saxifragaceae* are cultivated in landscape schemes. *Deutzia* are useful midsummer-flowering shrubs 1–2 m tall, with pink or pinkish-white flowers. Many species and hybrids are available, including *Deutzia scabra* and *Deutzia* × *elegantissima* 'Rosealind'.

Escallonia are evergreen shrubs with scented foliage suited to maritime areas, where they will take the full brunt of south-westerly winds. They are ideal as low windbreaks or hedges and as part of shrubberies. Some species and cultivars include:

Escallonia rubra, July, with pink flowers, foliage sticky to the touch
E. bifida, late summer, with white flowers
E. 'Apple Blossom', pale pink flowers
E. 'Slieve Donard', deep pink flowers

Hydrangea macrophylla, in the form of Hortensia (mop-headed) and lace cap hydrangeas are common shrubby garden plants, particularly in coastal areas. They also grow well in light woodland. In alkaline soil flowers are pink and in acidic soil conditions flowers are blue. Many cultivars are available.

Less common but useful as midsummer white-flowering shrubs are *Hydrangea quercifolia*, *H.* 'Annabelle' and *H. paniculata*. They are medium-sized, free-flowering shrubs and bloom in a period when few shrubs are in flower.

Hydrangea aspera Villosa Group and *H. aspera* subsp. *sargentiana* are striking for their large, densely hairy leaves, peeling bark and pinkish-mauve flowers in late summer.

H. anomala subsp. *petiolaris* is a fast-growing, easy-to-establish climber for a north-facing wall. Foliage is evergreen and heart-shaped and it is only when the corymbs of whitish flowers develop that a *Hydrangea* is clearly identifiable.

Philadelphus (mock orange) are deciduous shrubs flowering in midsummer. Flowers are white or white with a blotch of purple in the centre. They are often sweetly scented, hence the common name 'mock orange'. With the exception of *Philadelphus microphyllus*, which forms a low-domed hummock, they are larger than *Deutzia* by about a third. Many hybrids and cultivars have been raised, including *Philadelphus* 'Belle Etoile' with single flowers, each with a maroon blotch, *P.* 'Virginal', large-growing with double white flowers, and *P. coronarius* 'Aureus' with white flowers and golden-coloured foliage.

Ribes sanguineum (flowering currant) is a tough, hardy, deciduous shrub with pink flowers borne in spring. The shrub has rather a musty smell. Several cultivars have been raised including *R.* 'Pulborough Scarlet'.

Ribes speciosum is also deciduous. Fuchsia-like flowers, both in shape and colour, are borne on bare wood in late spring as the foliage emerges. This shrub is densely armed with thorns and is often trained against a wall in the early summer.

Ribes laurifolium, an evergreen ground-cover shrub, carries racemes of yellow flowers in February. It forms one of a number of early-spring yellow-flowering shrubs.

Other genera from the *Saxifragaceae* worth seeking in specialist nurseries are *Pileostegia* and *Schizophragma*, both climbers; *Itea ilicifolia*, evergreen shrubs with long racemes of greenish flowers in early winter; and *Carpenteria californica*, an evergreen white-flowered shrub for early summer.

Solanaceae **Potato**

This family provides several tender flowering shrubs for well-favoured situations. It also includes the food crops potato (*Solanum tuberosum*) and tomato (*Lycopersicon esculentum*). Green parts of the plants are poisonous.

TYPES OF PLANTS. Shrubs: medium size.
  Climbers: to several metres.

WORLD DISTRIBUTION. South America.

LEAVES. Foliage is alternate, entire, pinnate or lobed, evergreen, semi-deciduous or deciduous.

FLOWERS. Flower are borne in cymes. The corolla consists of a tube and five lobes, in the shape of a star in *Solanum* and funnel-shaped in *Cestrum*. Flower colour varies from mauve to red to white and yellow.

FRUIT. In *Solanum* fruit is yellowish white, like tiny tomatoes. In *Cestrum* it is described as a deep purple-red berry and is uncommon in cultivation.

GROWTH RATE AND LONGEVITY. In sheltered sites they are fast-growing shrubs.

FUNCTIONAL AND ORNAMENTAL USES
Shrubs for well-sheltered situations *Solanum* and *Cestrum*
Architectural foliage plants *Solanum laciniatum* and *S. rantonnetii*

GROWING CONDITIONS. Sheltered situations. Avoid windy sites as the foliage is thin and would be damaged by wind.

MANAGEMENT. In a sheltered site they grow rapidly and will require pruning when they outgrow their allotted space. *Solanum crispum* 'Glasnevin' can be cut back to within a few centimetres of ground level and it will regrow.

PARTICULAR PLANTING SCHEMES OR PLANT ASSOCIATIONS. *Cestrum fasciculatum* 'Newellii' is an evergreen shrub with an upright habit and tubular, dark red flowers.
  Solanum laxum 'Album' has become a common rampant climber, scrambling over fences in city gardens. White flowers are borne in late summer and early autumn.
  S. crispum 'Glasnevin' is vigorous shrub with mauve flowers requiring wall protection.
  Solanum laciniatum and *S. rantonnetii* are tender shrubs with striking architectural foliage, which are becoming more freely available in nursery catalogues. Both have deeply cut foliage and deep violet flowers with conspicuous yellow anthers, a pleasing combination.

Two other medium-sized shrubs worth seeking out for a well-drained soil in a dry situation are *Fabiana imbricata*, with white tubular flowers borne amid heather-like foliage in June, and *Vestia foetida*, with yellow tubular flowers borne in early summer.

———————————— • ————————————

Taxaceae Yew

Taxus (yew) is an evergreen tree with dark green linear leaves and red juicy fruit, known as arils. Trees are broad in outline, often broader than taller, especially if multi-stemmed. *Taxus* is poisonous in all its parts.

TYPES OF PLANTS. Trees: small- to medium-sized trees.
    Shrub: many cultivars of shrub-like proportions have been selected.

WORLD DISTRIBUTION. Europe, North Africa and western Asia. *Taxus* is native in Britain and Ireland.

LEAVES. Foliage is evergreen, linear, arranged in two ranks, deep green and ridged above and matt green and dull beneath, sharp pointed at the apex.

FLOWERS. Male and female trees occur. On the male trees, little globular 'flowers' are borne on the undersurface of the leaf; these open in March to release yellow pollen. Flowers on female trees are green and insignificant.

FRUIT. In late summer, seed encased in a red, fleshy, berry-like fruit, an aril, develops. The fruit remain on the trees until eaten by birds or until they fall to the ground.

BARK. This is often fluted and plum-coloured, though often not visible as it is covered in shoots.

GROWTH RATE AND LONGEVITY. *Taxus* is slow-growing and long-lived, up to 1000 years.

FUNCTIONAL AND ORNAMENTAL USES.
Specimen tree	*Taxus baccata*
Fastigiate upright tree	*T. baccata* 'Fastigiata' (Irish yew)
Ground cover shrub	*T. baccata* 'Semperaurea', *T. baccata* 'Dovastonia Aurea'
Evergreen golden-coloured shrub	*T. baccata* 'Semperaurea', *T. baccata* 'Dovastonia Aurea'
Topiary and hedging	*T. baccata*

GROWING CONDITIONS. *Taxus* grows well in shade and is often seen beneath tall trees.

MANAGEMENT. When grown as a hedge, it can be severely pruned, i.e. pruned to the trunk, and it will resprout within a few weeks. It is the only conifer that can be treated in such a manner. When grown as a tree, it requires little pruning. *Taxus* hedges require pruning two to three times per year.

PARTICULAR PLANTING SCHEMES OR PLANT ASSOCIATIONS. *Taxus* is native in Ireland and, while no longer abundant in the wild, place names such as Newry, County Down (*iúr*, yew tree), and Youghal, County Cork (*eo, coill, yew wood*), indicate the prominence it once had in the Irish landscape.

Taxus baccata 'Fastigiata' (Irish yew) is often planted in graveyards, for example, Glasnevin Cemetery, Dublin (Fig. 2.9).

At Mount Stewart, County Down, Northern Ireland, *Taxus* is to the fore in the shamrock garden. A yew hedge in the shape of a shamrock, a three-leaved clover, encloses the garden; at ground level a Red Hand of Ulster is created from stone and a focal point at the rear of the garden is a topiary Irish harp, created from *Taxus*, a touch of whimsy in a planting scheme.

Also in Belfast, Northern Ireland, an imposing avenue of *T. baccata* 'Fastigiata' (Irish yew), sweeps up a wide expanse of grass towards Stormont Castle.

T. baccata is planted in streets, parks and urban woodland in Central and Northern Europe (Saebø *et al.*, 2005).

Taxodiaceae Redwood

This family provides the largest and tallest-growing conifers in the world. The bark is often reddish brown in colour; hence the common name.

TYPES OF PLANTS. Large, long-lived trees to 30–40 m tall in cultivation.

WORLD DISTRIBUTION. Western North America, eastern North America, Japan and China.

LEAVES. Deciduous or evergreen in two ranks either side of a shoot, or scale-like leaves arranged into a whipcord (Table 4.30).

FLOWERS. Male strobili in clusters or panicles.

FRUIT. Cones, globose or ovoid.

BARK. Reddish-brown-coloured bark; often soft to the touch, is a feature of some genera in this family (Table 4.30).

GROWTH RATE AND LONGEVITY. Fast-growing and long-lived.

Table 4.30. Distinguishing features of genera in the *Taxodiaceae*.

Species	Common name	Habit	Size (m)	Bark/trunk	Foliage
Metasequoia glyptostroboides	Dawn cypress	Conical	20–25	Tapering, fluted trunk on older tree	Deciduous, individual leaflets are opposite
Sequoia sempervirens	Coast redwood	Conical	35–40	Thick soft bark	Flat hard foliage in two ranks
Sequoiadendron giganteum	Wellingtonia, giant redwood	Spire-like	45–50	Very thick, soft and fibrous	Tiny scale-like foliage arranged like a whipcord
Taxodium distichum	Swamp cypress	Dome-shaped with many fine branchlets	30–35	Pale brown, stringy	Deciduous, individual leaflets are alternate

FUNCTIONAL AND ORNAMENTAL USES.

Avenue trees	*Sequoiadendron giganteum*
Parkland	All genera
Specimen trees	All genera
Damp areas	*Taxodium* and *Metasequoia*

GROWING CONDITIONS. These trees are generally grown in parkland situations, where growing conditions are favourable.

MANAGEMENT. Given their long lifespan, care should be taken to give these trees sufficient space to grow and develop.

PARTICULAR PLANTING SCHEMES OR PLANT ASSOCIATIONS. *Metasequoia glyptostroboides* has an elegant conical habit, with shaggy peeling bark. The brown/orange-coloured, deeply fluted trunk is particularly noticeable in winter. The leaves are opposite, each leaf composed of tiny opposite leaflets (in *Taxodium* these leaflets are alternate). Autumn colour is pale yellow. Flower and fruit not observed. The conifer is not difficult to grow and is also fast-growing. It is being grown as a street tree in some European and American cities, an indication of a tough constitution. *M. glyptostroboides* has been in cultivation since 1948 and, in terms of conifers, it is only a pup.

Sequoia sempervirens (coast redwood) is evergreen, as the name indicates. The thick, soft bark is several centimetres thick and reddish brown in colour. In habit this tree is conical in shape, with long drooping branches upswept near their extremities. Foliage is dark green, two rows of linear leaves, which are stiff to the touch. This contrasts with *Larix* (larch) and *Taxus* (yew), which are softer to the touch. Male pollen is shed in late winter. Cones, 2 cm, globular in shape, are green and then mature to a red-brown colour.

Sequoia is the conifer with the greatest volume, whereas *Sequoiadendron* is taller.

Sequoiadendron giganteum is a tall, conical tree. At a distance these trees are readily identifiable because of their tall spire-like shape, dark green foliage and soft, deeply fissured bark. Individual leaves are scale-like and are arranged into cords of dark green shoots. The main branches curve upwards and then become somewhat drooping at the extremities of the branches. Male flowers shed their pollen in March or April. Cones, 8 cm × 5 cm on a 2 cm stalk, develop by late summer. The large, stalked cone also distinguishes *Sequoiadendron* from *Sequoia*.

At Scone, Perth, Scotland, examples of *S. giganteum*, grown from seed supplied by David Douglas, have become very large, awe-inspiring trees. In the late 19th century, avenues of *Sequoiadendron* were planted in rural estates and in large suburban gardens of the period. Remnants of such avenues remain in lands that have since become public parks and housing estates.

Taxodium distichum (swamp cypress), a deciduous conifer, has a pale reddish-brown bark, often stringy. Conical in shape, it has a domed apex and a mass of branches. With dense branches and the appearance of new-growth pale green leaves in early summer, the tree looks rather 'fuzzy'. The side shoots have alternate ranks of foliage, which in turn are alternate (in *Metasequoia* the 'leaflets' are opposite and in turn have opposite 'leaves'). In autumn the foliage turns a rich fox-red.

Specimens growing by water produce pneumatomaphores, commonly called 'knees', which help aerate the roots. A striking example occurred at the National Botanic Gardens of Belgium, Meise, near Brussels, where these 'knees' stretched for more than a metre and attained a height of many centimetres.

In the Parque de Retiro, Madrid, a large specimen towers over a formal parterre garden. By the Palacio de Crystal in the same garden, several specimens stand in water and imbue the common name, swamp cypress, with a fuller meaning.

Tiliaceae Lime

A family of trees and shrubs and some non-woody plants of *Tilia*, it is widely planted as deciduous street, parkland and avenue trees.

TYPES OF PLANTS. Trees: medium to large to very large long-lived trees. Depending on the species, they become large (30–40 m tall). Younger trees are loosely conical in outline, becoming more dome-shaped with ascending and then down-curved branches as they mature.

WORLD DISTRIBUTION. Europe, China, North America.

LEAVES. Foliage is deciduous, alternate, often cordate in shape and oblique at the base. The leaves are thin in texture, some with tufts of orange hairs in the axils of the leaves (Fig. 4.15). In winter the twigs of *Tilia* are red and are noticeable when lit by winter sun. Winter buds are ovoid, smooth to the touch and red or green in colour.

FLOWERS. The inflorescence, borne in early summer, is composed of an elliptically shaped bract and yellow, scented flowers, which hang below the leaves. The fragrance of the flowers is noticeable on a hot summer's day.

FRUIT. Fruit are ovoid, nut-like, clothed in hairs and, together with the bract, are shed in autumn.

BARK. The bark is smooth to slightly fissured, pale to dark grey in colour.

GROWTH RATE AND LONGEVITY. *Tilia* grow and establish quickly. They are long-lived trees, surviving for 150–200 years.

FUNCTIONAL AND ORNAMENTAL USES (Table 4.31). Avenue planting and parkland trees.
    Street and urban park trees (in the USA *Tilia* would be described as a shade tree).
    Pleached trees: 'a hedge on stilts'. Pleached trees can now be purchased from some European nurseries.

GROWING CONDITIONS. They thrive in good soil and should not be planted in windswept conditions. They withstand low temperatures.

MANAGEMENT. Suckering at the base of the trunk is a feature of *Tilia* × *euchlora* and *T.* × *europaea*. Where space is limited the suckers are removed.

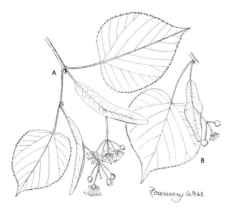

Fig. 4.15. (A) *Tilia platyphyllos*, large-leaved lime; (B) *Tilia cordata*, small-leaved lime. (From Savill, 1991.)

PESTS AND DISEASES. Where lime leaf aphid (*Eucallipterus tiliae*) infests trees, cars and street furniture can become covered in honeydew and sooty moulds. In Dublin, horse chestnut scale insect (*Pulvinaria regalis*) is becoming widespread on *Tilia* and the debilitating effect of the insect on the tree is noticeable.

PARTICULAR PLANTING SCHEMES OR PLANT ASSOCIATIONS. The genus is widely planted in cities in Southern, Central and Northern Europe (Saebø *et al.*, 2005).
    Since the 17th century the 1-km long, tree-lined boulevard, Unter den Linden, Berlin, has been one of the set pieces of

Table 4.31. Main taxa of *Tilia* (lime) and their uses in landscape schemes.

Genus and species name	Common name	Height (m)	Tree shape	Leaf size	Use
Tilia americana		30	Tall open dome	10–20 cm long	Specimen tree
Tilia cordata	Small-leaved lime	30	Tall dense dome	4–7 cm × 3–5 cm, large buff or orange tufts in axils	Street tree, avenue tree
T. cordata 'Böhjle'		20	Dome with upswept branches		Street tree
T. cordata 'Glenleven'		30			Street tree
T. cordata 'Greenspire'		20	Conical outline		Street tree
Tilia × *euchlora*	Caucausian lime	18–20		5–10 cm long	Parkland tree
Tilia × *europaea*	Common lime	40	Tall, broadly dome-shaped	6–10 cm long, white or buff tufts in axils	Avenue tree, parkland tree
Tilia × *europaea* 'Pallida'	Kaiser linden	30	Broadly conical		Avenue tree, street tree
Tilia platyphyllos	Large-leaved lime	30	Narrow, dome-shaped	6–15 cm × 6–15 cm, pubescent above and below	Parkland tree
Tilia tomentosa	Silver lime	25	Broadly dome-shaped	12–15 cm, densely pubescent beneath	Parkland tree
T. tomentosa 'Brabant'			Broadly conical		Street tree

urban street tree planting in Europe. Originally planted with *Juglans* and *Tilia*, it is now planted solely with *Tilia*.

In Paris, pleached lime accentuates the formality of the Palais Royal.

Tilia (lime) avenues are a feature of many estates in Ireland and Britain. Some examples of mature avenues are Ham House, Richmond, near London, Pollock Park, Glasgow and Clongowes Wood, Clane, County Kildare, Ireland. The recently replanted avenues lining the Long Water at Hampton Court, near London, will continue such a feature long into the future.

In recent years Danish tree breeders have been selecting new cultivars, *Tilia* 'Odin', *T.* × *euchlora* 'Frigg' and *T. platyphyllos* 'Fenris', for use in avenues and parks (Brander, 1995).

In the early 20th century, Chinese *Tilia*, such as *T. oliveri*, *T. chingiana* and *T. henryana*, with large leaves, were introduced from China. They become attractive trees and are worth seeking out in specialist tree nurseries for cultivation in parkland situations.

Ulmaceae Elm

Trees were once common in Europe but many were wiped out by Dutch elm disease. In Britain and Ireland many stumps have resprouted and have developed into bushy trees. Foliage rough to the touch and oblique at the base often indicates an *Ulmus* (elm).

TYPES OF PLANTS. Trees: medium to large.

WORLD DISTRIBUTION. Western Asia, North America and Europe, including England (some species).

LEAVES. Foliage is alternate, deciduous, sometimes hairy and rough to the touch. Margins of the leaves are toothed, usually in two sizes (Fig. 4.16).

FLOWERS. Dense clusters of flowers with conspicuous stamens develop in spring before the foliage unfolds.

FRUIT. Clusters of fruit develop in early summer. Each fruit is winged, a seed encircled by a paper-like membrane.

BARK. Bark is often dark brown and fissured into square plates.

GROWTH RATE AND LONGEVITY. They are quick to establish. Longevity is an issue. Trees develop for 10–15 years and then succumb to Dutch elm disease. Some resistant hybrids have been selected but how long they remain resistant is unclear.

FUNCTIONAL AND ORNAMENTAL USES.
Avenue tree
Street tree   *Ulmus* 'Clusius', *U.* 'Dodoens' and *U.* × *hollandica* 'Lobel'

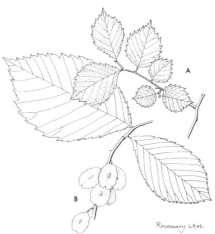

Fig. 4.16. (A) *Ulmus procera*, English elm; (B) *Ulmus glabra*, wych elm. (From Savill, 1991.)

GROWING CONDITIONS. *Ulmus* will grow in windswept areas and in poor soil conditions. When planting, areas where Dutch elm disease has occurred should be avoided.

MANAGEMENT. Dutch elm disease (*Ceratocystus ulmi*) is carried by an elm bark beetle (*Scolytus scolytus*); trees survive until they are attacked again. Bark beetles carry spores of the disease from the bark of an infected tree to a healthy tree. *Ulmus* regenerates after pruning and it can be very difficult to eradicate as it continues to send up shoots.

PARTICULAR PLANTING SCHEMES OR PLANT ASSOCIATIONS. *Ulmus* × *hollandica* 'Lobel' are planted in a car park in Almera, the Netherlands (Fig. 1.2).

In parts of inner-city Dublin, some specimens of *Ulmus* planted as street trees have attained a height of some 12 m and have a healthy appearance.

In central and Southern Europe, *Ulmus* is much used as a street tree, and in Northern Europe it is used to some extent (Saebø *et al.*, 2005).

Vitaceae Vine

This is the only family among landscape trees and shrubs for temperate regions where all members are climbers. These climbers have tendrils, a thread-like appendage that allows a climber to coil around a support as it grows. *Vitis vinifera* is the vine of commerce, known for grapes and wine.

TYPES OF PLANTS. Climbers up to several metres in length.

WORLD DISTRIBUTION. Northern hemisphere (*Vitis*); subtropics and tropics (*Cissus*), North America, Himalaya and Eastern Asia (*Parthenocissus*) and North America and Asia (*Ampelopsis*).

LEAVES. Foliage is opposite or alternate deciduous or evergreen (*Cissus striata*), Foliage is simple or compound, some leaves adapted into tendrils.

Ampelopsis: three- to five-lobed leaves.
Cissus: five glossy green leaflets.
Parthenocissus: leaves digitate, three to five leaflets.
Vitis: leaves palmately lobed.

FLOWERS. While individual flowers are small, the overall inflorescence is noticeable, though not striking.

FRUIT. Dark blue-black fruit occur on *Vitis* – the familiar grape; *Parthenocissus* and *Cissus* have clusters of blackcurrant-like fruit.

GROWTH RATE AND LONGEVITY. Fast to very fast. They are long-lived. *Cissus* is very fast-growing.

FUNCTIONAL AND ORNAMENTAL USES.
To cover walls and pergolas
To cover unsightly objects
Autumn colour   *Parthenocissus*
Fast-growing climbers   *Cissus striata, Parthenocissus henryana,*
                                                      P. quinquefolia

GROWING CONDITIONS. With *Ampelopsis*, a long, hot summer is required before flowers and fruit develop.

MANAGEMENT. *Parthenocissus* attaches itself to a wall by sucker pads. *Vitis, Cissus* and *Ampelopsis* attach themselves to supports or to other plants.

Where they are grown as wall shrubs, *V. vinifera* are trained as pruned vines. Others are pruned severely every few years and will grow again.

PARTICULAR PLANTING SCHEMES OR PLANT ASSOCIATIONS. Marvellous specimens of *Vitis coignetiae* occur at the Talbot Botanic Gardens, Malahide Castle, Dublin, and National Arboretum, Castlewellan, Northern Ireland. Leaves the size of dinner plates sprawl over the surrounding vegetation.

Parthenocissus henryana, with purple, marbled foliage, is one of the few species with purple-coloured foliage. It is a fast-growing climber and looks well against a whitewashed wall.

P. quinquefolia (virginia creeper) and *P. tricuspidata* (Boston ivy) are commonly grown climbers clothing walls of older houses in rural and urban areas. They produce stunning autumn colour in shades of red and amber.

References

Arnold-Foster, W. (1948) *Shrubs for the Milder Counties.* Country Life, London [2000 edition published by Alison Hodge, Bosulval, Newmill, Penzance, UK.]

Bean, W.J. (1970–1980) *Trees and Shrubs Hardy in the British Isles,* 8th edn. John Murray, London.

Brander, P.E. (1995) *Tilia* (lind) til alléer, aprk og anlæg – et alternative til elm. *Grøn viden* 88 (September), 1–6. [In Danish.]

Cullen, J. (2001) *Handbook of European Garden Plants.* Cambridge University Press, Cambridge.

Forrest, M. (2004) The introduction of oak species into Britain and Ireland. *International Oaks* 15, 82–93.

Halpenny, K. and Simms, W. (2005) The national collection of shrubby potentillas at Ardgillan Demesne, Balbriggan, Co. Dublin. *Moorea* 14, 17–22.

Jablonskii, E. (2004) European oak cultivars, collections and collectors. *International Oaks* 15, 103–118.

Saebø, A., Borzan,Ž., Ducatillion, C., Hatzistathis, A., Lagerström, T., Supuka, J., Garcia-Valdecantos, J.L., Rego, F. and Van Slycken, J. (2005) The selection of plant materials for street trees, park trees and urban woodland. In: Konijnendijk, C., Nilsson, K., Randrup, T. and Schipperijn, J. (eds) (2005) *Urban Forests and Trees.* Springer, Berlin, pp. 257–280.

Savill, P. (1991) *The Silviculture of Trees Used in British Forestry.* CAB International, Wallingford, UK.

Tello, M.-L., Tomalek, M., Siwecki, R., Gáper, J., Motta, E. and Mateo-Sagasta, E. (2005) Biotic urban growing conditions – threats, pests and diseases. In: Konijnendijk, C., Nilsson, K., Randrup, T. and Schipperijn, J. (eds) *Urban Forests and Trees.* Springer, Berlin, pp. 325–365.

Further Reading

Argent, G., Bond, J., Chamberlain, D., Cox, P. and Hardy, A. (1997) *The Rhododendron Handbook 1998.* The Royal Horticultural Society, London.

Cappiello, P. and Shadow, D. (2005) *Dogwoods: The Genus Cornus.* Timber Press, Portland, Oregon.

Chadbund, G. (1972) *Flowering Cherries.* Collins, London.

Fiala, J. (1995) *Flowering Crabapples: The Genus Malus.* Timber Press, Portland, Oregon.

Fiala, J. (2002) *Lilacs: The Genus Syringa.* Timber Press, Portland, Oregon.

Galle, F.C. (1997) *Hollies: The Genus Ilex.* Timber Press, Portland, Oregon.

Gardiner, J. (2000) *Magnolias: A Gardener's Guide.* Timber Press, Portland, Oregon.

Lane, C. (2005) *Witch Hazels.* Timber Press, Portland, Oregon.

Mitchell, A. (2001) *Collins Field Guide: Trees of Britain and Northern Europe.* Collins, London.

Newsholme, C. (2003) *Willows, The Genus Salix.* Timber Press, Portland, Oregon.

Phillips, R. and Rix, M. (2004) *Ultimate Guide to Roses: A Comprehensive Selection.* Macmillan, London.

Phipps, J. (2003) *Hawthorns and Medlars.* Timber Press, Portland, Oregon.

Treseder, N. (1978) *Magnolias.* Faber & Faber, London.

Underhill, D. (1971) *Heaths and Heathers.* David and Charles, Newton Abbot, UK.

Upson, T. and Andrews, S. (2004) *The Genus Lavandula.* Royal Botanic Gardens, Kew, London.

Van Gelderen, C.J. and Van Gelderen, D.M. (1999) *Maples for Gardens.* Timber Press, Portland, Oregon.

Van Gelderen, D.M., de Jong, P.C. and Oterdoom, H.J. (1994) *Maples of the World,* Timber Press, Portland, Oregon.

Vertrees, J.D. and Gregory, P. (2001) *Japanese Maples.* Timber Press, Portland, Oregon.

5 Designing with Trees and Shrubs

The words plants, plant material and vegetation are used interchangeably in the literature to denote one of the materials of landscape design. The other materials are landform, water, sculptural forms, buildings, site structures (e.g. walls) and ground pattern (e.g. pavement). Crowe in *Garden Design* (1994) writes: 'It is impossible to have too great a range of plants to choose from, provided a choice is made.' Drawing on the families described in Chapter 4, this chapter examines the development of planting schemes with trees and shrubs.

'Few of the plants are unusual, but it is the way that they are used that make the individual gardens and borders what they are' (Bird, 1994). While this comment refers to the design of a private garden, Dalemain, near Penrith, Cumbria, it can also be applied to the work of landscape designers as they design large-scale planting schemes. Planting design is a process through which a design concept is developed for a particular site and then, based on the design concept, a particular planting scheme, composition, assemblage or structure is developed. Planting design is generally part of a larger process of landscape design where a landscape architect is working to a client's design brief.

Factors Influencing the Development of a Planting Scheme

Scale and situation

The terms structure planting, amenity planting and detailed ornamental planting used by Robinson (2004) reflect the different scales of planting seen in present-day landscape situations. Examples of structure planting are seen on motorways, where large numbers of trees and shrubs have been planted, creating corridors of woodland. Amenity planting is seen in shopping centres,

© M. Forrest 2006. *Landscape Trees and Shrubs: Selection, Use and Management*
(M. Forrest)

business parks and public open spaces, where swathes of shrubs with some trees provide visual interest for users of the area (Fig. 5.1). Detailed ornamental planting is seen close to high-profile buildings, in courtyard gardens, within office or apartment complexes and in private gardens.

In developing a planting design, the overall situation or location of the scheme must be considered. 'To my mind the antithesis of good gardening is to try to force upon a resisting district the growth of plants that are naturally incapable of survival and that are therefore out of place and context.' While Derek Hill (1968) was writing about his rural garden in Donegal, north-west Ireland, which is surrounded by lakes and mountains, his judgement is applicable to present-day landscape schemes, be they in urban or rural locations. In a rural area, where dome-shaped deciduous parkland trees such as *Fagus sylvatica* punctuate the skyline, the introduction of fastigiate *Populus nigra* 'Italica' might not be appropriate. The treatment of a roundabout in a city centre and in a rural area may be totally different, either in the type of plants that would be grown or in the manner in which they are designed or managed.

Site conditions

'They took to the earth and smiled.' So wrote an artist about her recently planted *Acer palmatum* (Japanese maples). While not the language of

Fig. 5.1. Large-scale amenity planting in Newcastle upon Tyne, England.

technical instructions, none the less it is a necessary outcome of any planting plan. For plants to survive and ideally thrive, adequate moisture and light levels are required. If a plant struggles, is under stress and does not grow satisfactorily, then it becomes more susceptible to pests and diseases.

Above-ground conditions of light, wind and existing vegetation must be taken into account. Too little light and a plant becomes etiolated, with long internodes and poor leaf and flower development. Too much light and foliage is scorched. Orientation of the site can also affect plant selection. Where winter frosts occur, plants in an easterly facing site can be damaged by early morning sun, whereas those in a westerly facing site are not.

Where wind is more or less constant, it can be almost impossible to establish vegetation and what will grow is moulded by the prevailing wind. A maritime area has the advantage of a longer growing season than an inland site, but it has the disadvantage of being windier and salt-laden winds can damage certain plants. In an apparently sheltered West Cork garden, within view of an inlet of the sea, a row of *Betula utilis* was under planted with *Cornus alba*; part of the scheme grew luxuriantly, another did not. In a large Dublin shopping centre, mass plantings of *Choisya ternata* were damaged by cold winds in an exposed part of the site and grew well where they were in the protection of buildings. Even in a small site, variation in growing conditions, in these cases caused by wind, can affect a designer's intention.

Existing vegetation on a site can be a bonus or a bane. On the one hand, it provides a ready-made structure, which can be enhanced or removed as a new scheme develops. It provides shelter and protection for the newer plants. On the other hand, it can be difficult to establish young plants in the shade of existing vegetation, where they have to struggle for light and moisture. However, the advantages of existing trees and shrubs on a site usually far outweigh the disadvantages.

Soil

Existing soil conditions must be considered and can determine what kind of vegetation can be cultivated on the site. Topsoil is a fine balance of soil particles and open pores. These pores are filled with air and water, both of which are necessary for soil fungi and bacteria but also for the growth of roots. Too much water in a soil and it becomes waterlogged and roots die; too little air in the soil, when it becomes compacted, and the roots die. Soil particles are composed of sand, silt and clay. A simple soil test allows one to check the soil type. A squeezed handful of sandy soil will not bind together and will feel gritty to the touch. Such soils are free-draining but will not retain moisture. A handful of clay soil is malleable like a piece of putty. Silty soils are sticky to the touch, can be difficult to cultivate, will dry out in drought and become waterlogged after rainfall. Methods of assessment of soils for use in landscape situations are described by Trowbridge and Bassuk (2004). Topsoil also contains plant nutrients necessary for plant growth: nitrogen, potassium, phosphorus, with minor elements of calcium and magnesium.

Availability of moisture in the soil or the atmosphere is another site consideration. Too much moisture in the soil and waterlogging occurs, roots are damaged and the plant suffers and dies. Too little moisture in the soil and drought occurs and a plant wilts and eventually dies. Some plants of their nature thrive in damp sites, e.g. *Salix* (willow) and other members of the *Salicaceae*; others do not, e.g. *Griselinia* (*Cornaceae*) and members of the *Cistaceae*. Some prefer high levels of misty rain, e.g. *Rhododendron*, whereas, for example, *Brachyglottis* does not.

Soil pH is another factor. A great range of plants grow in soils of pH 5.7–6.7. If acidic conditions (pH 3–5) prevail, as in boggy or peaty conditions, then plant selection is largely based on the *Ericaceae*, e.g. *Rhododendron* and *Pieris*. If alkaline conditions (pH 7–8.5) occur, as in the chalk soils of the south of England, some members of the *Rosaceae* are suitable for cultivation.

In urban areas soil conditions and growing conditions in general can vary greatly from the surrounding countryside. Soil in cities is often compacted, poorly drained, atypical, often formed from rubble, sub-soil and soil of mixed origin having been brought on site from other locations. The effect of a variation in soil quality is noticeable where one species is cultivated in large numbers, as in a lengthy hedge; some sections thrive, others do not. Within an urban area, rain shadows can occur, limiting the availability of moisture for vegetation. Light levels can also be lower in streets with tall buildings than in the surrounding suburban areas, causing etiolated or stunted growth in trees (Bassuk and Whitlow, 1988). Where winter conditions are severe and de-icing salts are applied to roads and pavements, surrounding vegetation is damaged by excess salts in the soil and growth rate is reduced. For further discussion about urban growing conditions, see Trowbridge and Bassuk (2004), *Trees in the Urban Landscape: Site Assessment, Design, and Installation* and Bradshaw *et al.* (1995), *Trees in the Urban Landscape: Principles and Practice*. In *Some Branch against the Sky*, Dutton (1997), in describing his garden on a marginal site in Scotland, 275 m altitude and 57° latitude, provides useful advice on the development of any marginal site.

'Adaptability to existing conditions and the power to see and use the natural beauties of the ground to the greatest advantage are essential to success' (Waterfield, 1907). This holds true 100 years later, be it a garden in an industrial town or a coastal amenity site.

Development of a planting scheme

Having considered the site, the scheme is further developed.

What is the function of the scheme? For example, an avenue linking one building with another or an interior patio to be viewed from offices and accessible for passive recreation.

Are there particular requirements from the public or a particular client? School grounds, where the plants may be used for educational purposes, are examples.

When is the scheme to mature? In present-day planting schemes, the usual estimate is 3–5 years. Depending on the size of trees planted, it may take 15–20 years before an avenue of *Quercus* (oak) or *Tilia* (lime) develops a sense of maturity.

What is the scale of the scheme? A few metres in a city apartment block or several kilometres of railway embankment.

What effect is to be created? A woodland, a pattern of neat shrubs, a space with a few plants or a space filled with plants, a dense barrier and so on.

What type of vegetation can be cultivated to achieve the desired effect? Tall trees, dwarf shrubs, wild flowers, shrubs with bold variegated foliage and so on.

Plant associations

Planting with foresight and grouping plants together are skills that are developed over time. In a large site, where immediate effect is not of the essence, some slower-growing trees could be planted that would outlive the designer by many generations. The work of Capability Brown at Blenheim, Oxfordshire, or Daniel Marot at Hampton Court Palace, near London, comes to mind.

'I have treated flowers not as a single specimens, but in relation to their setting of house or wall, lawn or woodland, or as a foreground to the landscape, planned for the beauty of the whole effect' (Waterfield, 1907). While written in the context of flowers in a garden, the idea of 'beauty of the whole effect' could, in terms of present-day landscape situations, be substituted with the words sustainability, robustness, reliability, functionality as well as the beauty of the whole effect.

Landscape designers develop a capacity to see in their mind's eye how a scheme will develop over the years in the medium and long term, in much the same way as composers 'hear' their composition in their head. Too much of the same plant may look well aesthetically but may be even-aged, will have to be removed at the same time and is more vulnerable to a pest or disease attack. A balance is struck between diversity and monotony, what is aesthetically pleasing and what will provide ecological interest.

Post-planting management

Issues related to post-planting management also influence the design of a planting scheme. Are resources available for the maintenance of the scheme in the short and long term so that the design intention can be achieved? Trees require formative pruning, hedges need regular trimming, ground-cover schemes must be maintained weed- and litter-free. Rose gardens are much appreciated by the general public but they are labour-intensive, a management issue to be considered at the design stage.

Plants require water. Will an irrigation system be installed or will rainfall supply sufficient moisture? Weeds develop and compete with trees and shrubs for nutrients and moisture. Trees and shrubs grow and will require pruning. Some plants grow faster than others and outgrow their allotted space. Are staff available to prune or remove the shrubs?

As the saying goes, 'Where a plant grows well and looks well can be two different places.' The key to good planting design and management is to match the two as closely as possible. In present-day landscape situations, amending or ameliorating the growing conditions is usually only possible in limited situations and on a small rather than a large scale.

Plants in a scheme

Having refined a planting design, particular plants are selected for the scheme in question. The Irish author and playwright Bryan McMahon wrote in *The Master* (1992):

> In a well made play, every sentence must convey one of three things, possibly two or all three together, that is, if the playwright is talented or lucky: every comment must advance the plot, throw light on character or raise a laugh.

A similar question could be asked as to why each tree or shrub is proposed for a particular scheme.

Based on his experience of developing a woodland garden at Dargle Cottage, County Wicklow, Ireland, Sir Basil Goulding (1982) advised taking a shrub catalogue and listing plants under columns labelled 'chorus' and 'soloist'. Form and texture differentiate the two categories and he gives examples of *Syringa* (lilac) and *Acer* (maple), which he describes as follows:

> the form of a lilac bush is practically non-existent; it has indefinacy, drab dullness (when not flowering: i.e. usually) and no arresting character. The form of maple by contrast, is that of a principal actor – arresting, elegant, soignée, versatile and essentially personified.

He then describes how the 'choral' shrubs are suitable for massing on their own or with other choral shrubs and the 'soloists' 'need to be lime-lighted before a backcloth of choral plants'. Taking these definitions a little further, plant too many 'soloists' together and the effect can be lost. For example, one well-sited *Fraxinus excelsior* 'Pendula' or *Fagus sylvatica* 'Pendula' can look stunning, but put them in a group and the effect is funereal and eerie. Much planting in landscape schemes could be described as 'chorus', but taking the analogy a little further, it could be contrasted with a jazz band where different instruments are featured during a piece, clarinet, saxophone, drums and so on. In a similar way, a planting scheme of evergreen shrubs would 'feature' *Viburnum tinus*, flowering in winter, *Prunus laurocerasus*, flowering in early summer, *Cotoneaster lacteus*, with red berries in autumn, against the regular drum beat of *Aucuba japonica* 'Variegata', an evergreen variegated shrub.

Characteristics of each plant

Some trees are slow-growing and long-lived, e.g. *Taxus baccata* (yew). Others are fast-growing and relatively short-lived, e.g. members of the *Salicaceae*. The ground cover *Rubus tricolor* is fast-growing and is suitable for a large area, but *R. rolfei*, being slower-growing and with neater foliage, would be more suitable for a small space. In connection with growth rate, it is useful to consider the shape and habit of trees and shrubs and how that alters over the lifetime of a plant (Chapter 2) and what effect this would have on the functional and aesthetic roles of the planting design. An exercise examining the growth rate of shrubs is given at the end of this chapter.

The selection of ornamental features, such as flower and fruit, is to some extent determined by what is in flower or fruit at that time of year. In spring, yellow is the dominant flower colour among shrubs, *Jasminum nudiflorum*, *Hamamelis*, *Mahonia*, *Forsythia*, *Kerria*, followed by rhododendrons in all colours except blue, pinks of *Prunus* (cherries) and *Malus* (apples), then moving to summer whites of *Crataegus*, (hawthorn), *Sorbus* (rowan), *Philadelphus* and *Choisya* and to autumn red and orange berries of *Pyracantha*, *Cotoneaster* and *Sorbus* and autumn colours of *Acer* and *Betula*.

Some plants have specific horticultural requirements, which have to be noted. Some have particular soil requirements, e.g. *Ericaceae*. If berries are required on *Skimmia* or *Ilex* (holly), then male and female plants must be specified. If *Forsythia* is grown for its yellow spring flowers, then it must be noted that pruning after flowering is necessary.

Purchasing plants from a nursery

When preparing a planting design, nursery catalogues are a valuable source of information. Catalogues list the prices and sizes of plants supplied by a nursery and in some cases give a brief description of these plants. Several categories of nursery stock are supplied by nurseries (Table 5.1).

Transplants are seedlings that have been transplanted a number of times and are usually 20–60 cm tall. The numbers 2 + 1 or 2 + 2 are used to indicate that the transplants have been in a seed bed for 2 years followed by 1 or 2 years in a transplant line. Whips have a single leader and are usually available in sizes of 60–90 cm and 90–120 cm tall. With feathered trees the side branches or 'feathers' are retained to ground level. Standard trees are so called because of their clear bole to 1.8 m. Depending on the girth of the tree, measured at 1 m above ground level, standard trees are further described as light standards, standards, heavy standards and extra heavy standards. Semi-mature trees are grown in a nursery until they attain a height of 10–12 m (Fig. 2.5) (James, 1990) or with a girth of 25–30 cm, 30–35 cm, 35–40 cm and so on (Wilson *et al.*, 2004). Multi-stem trees have two to three trunks arising close to ground level (Fig. 4.2). Shrubs are also multi-stemmed, with several main stems and many lateral branches. Depending on the size of the shrubs, they are sold in pot sizes of various dimensions from 2 to 10 litres.

Table 5.1. Types of nursery stock available from nurseries.

Types of nursery stock	Situations where they are cultivated
Transplants	Motorways, reclamation sites, urban woodland
Whips	Motorways, reclamation sites, urban woodland
Feathered trees	Specimen trees, parkland trees
Standards	Street trees, amenity trees in parks, specimens in association with shrubs
Multi-stem tree	Specimen trees where space permits, barrier planting
Semi-mature trees	Specimen trees in civic spaces

Further information about plant sizes is given in the National Plant Specification (HTA, 2002). Costs of plants will vary with size; for instance, a 150 cm tall transplant of *Acer platanoides* might cost 40 pence when purchased bare rooted and in bulk, whereas a root-balled tree with a girth of 10–12 cm might cost £20 and a semi-mature tree £1000.

When placing an order, it is worthwhile visiting a nursery and checking the quality of the stock on sale. Select well-shaped, well-rooted, healthy plants. Avoid plants that are pot-bound. They will never 'root out' into soil; misshapen in the case of shrubs or without a clear leader in the case of trees, they rarely develop into well-shaped plants. Avoid trees or shrubs showing signs of pests and diseases. Indicators of quality given by McKay (1997) are as follows: condition of large woody roots, quantity of large woody roots, sturdiness, i.e. stem height divided by stem diameter, condition of fine roots, quantity of fine and lateral roots and shoot moisture content. Some purchasers tag their selected plants and specify how they are to be packed and dispatched to the site for planting.

Plant spacing is another challenging topic. The numbers of plants specified in a contract document will depend on the cost of the plants, the size of plants specified, growth rate of the selected plants, the site and in particular the growing conditions. If plants will grow fast in that location, then few plants are required. If they are slow growing in the site, then more plants are required. When is the scheme to mature? If a shopping centre is opening in a few weeks' time and landscape contractors are gaining access to the site with the opening ceremony imminent, then plant spacing would be closer than if plants had a number of months to mature. Two rules of thumb for plant spacing of shrubs are recommended: where the ultimate height is 1 m, then plant 1 m apart, or where a 2 m wide shrub is grown alongside a 1 m wide shrub, plant them at 1.5 m apart (known as planting centre) (Jakobsen, 1990).

Trees: Selection, Use and Management

Parkland trees

Parkland trees are long-lived trees (up to 250 years or more), 25–38/40 m tall at maturity. They are planted to create woodland, avenues, as parkland specimens or perimeter planting on large estates (Fig. 2.2). Their sheer shape and size make an impact on the landscape and some are known for their flower and fruit, *Aesculus* and *Fagus,* for example. Depending on the location of a proposed planting scheme, whips and transplants, feathered or standard trees of various girths and semi-mature trees are planted. A list of plant families which for the most part are large-growing trees and includes deciduous parkland trees is given in Table 5.2. A list of parkland species is given in Appendix 1.

Conifers

Coniferous trees are primarily evergreen with a number of deciduous genera such as *Larix* (larch) and *Taxodium* (swamp cypress). A number occur in parkland situations, some are grown in parks and open spaces – amenity parks, particularly in Southern and Eastern Europe rather than Western Europe. Smaller-growing conifers are popular in suburban gardens. Table 5.3 lists the common families of conifers grown in landscape schemes.

Table 5.2. Families of large trees for parkland and woodland schemes.

Family	Common name	Deciduous/ evergreen	Identification	Some native species	Common function	Poor soil conditions
Aceraceae	Maple	D	Opposite leaves, samara seed	X	Street tree, ornamental tree	X
Betulaceae	Birch	D	Alternate leaf, catkins	X	Street tree, ornamental tree	X
Fagaceae	Beech, oak	D	Alternate leaf, pointed buds	X	Parkland, specimen	
Hippocastanaceae	Horse chestnut	D	Alternate leaf, white flowers, 'conkers'	X	Parkland, avenues	
Juglandaceae	Walnut	D	Pinnate leaves, alternate		Parkland tree, ornamental tree	
Magnoliaceae	Magnolia, tulip tree	D/E	Large leaves, striking flowers		Ornamental tree in well-favoured site	
Platanaceae	Plane	D	Alternate leaves, flower/fruit		Street trees, park tree, avenue,	
Salicaceae	Willow and poplar	D	Alternate leaves	X	Soil stabilization	X
Tiliaceae	Lime	D	Alternate leaves, small yellow flowers		Street tree, avenue, parkland tree	
Ulmaceae	Elm	D	Alternate leaves, rough to the touch	X	Street tree	

Table 5.3. Families of coniferous trees and shrubs.

Family	Common name	Tree	Shrubs	Identification	Some native species	Maritime areas	Common function	Poor soil conditions	Deciduous/ evergreen
Cupressaceae	Cypress	X	X	Very tiny leaves, cones	X	Some	Ornamental trees, shelter belts	X (some)	E
Ginkgoaceae	Maidenhair tree	X		Leaves shaped like those of a maidenhair fern			Specimen tree, street tree		D
Pinaceae	Pine	X	X	Needle-like foliage in clusters, cones	X	Some	Specimen trees, shelter belts	X (some)	E/D
Taxaceae	Yew	X	Some cultivars	Dark green soft, needle-like leaves, red fruit	X		Specimen, native schemes, hedge, fastigiate tree	X	E
Taxodiaceae	Sequoia, swamp cypress	X		Needle-like foliage, very large trees			Specimen trees		E/D

Street trees

Street trees refer to trees that line roads in urban areas. As discussed earlier, urban conditions are harsh and inhospitable for tree growth and development. The average mortality of standard trees in urban areas was 50% (Peters, 1987) and in their first 3 years 23% died and another 16% in the subsequent 2 years (Gilbertson and Bradshaw, 1990), both cited by McEvoy and McKay (1997). In Britain and Ireland, standard trees with columnar shape, lollipop shape or V-shape are commonly used as street trees. In continental European cities, streets are lined with larger-growing trees such as *Platanus* and *Tilia*. In a survey concerning tree establishment in 17 European countries, three to five genera accounted for 50–70% of all street trees planted. The most common genera planted were *Tilia, Malus, Platanus, Aesculus, Quercus* and *Fraxinus* (Pauliet *et al.*, 2002). Street trees are planted in individual planting pits, continuous planting pits or grass margins. Street trees are either bare-rooted, container-grown or root-balled (where the root-ball has been lifted and wrapped in a protective wrapping). Issues such as underground services, soil type, the availability of moisture and the potential impact of roots on surrounding pavements and kerbs must be taken into consideration (Bradshaw *et al.*, 1995; Edwards and Gale, 2004; Trowbridge and Bassuk, 2004).

Many of the street trees are selected forms of trees in families of parkland trees listed in Table 5.2. e.g. *Tilia* 'Greenspire' (*Tiliaceae*) and *Acer platanoides* 'Columnare' (*Aceraceae*). Members of the *Rosaceae, Sorbus, Crataegus* and some *Prunus* species are commonly planted street trees (Fig. 4.11).

Semi-mature trees

Semi-mature trees some 10–12 m or more tall create an 'instant effect' and bring a landscape design from a drawing to reality in the time it takes to obtain and plant the tree. However, such trees are very costly and require particular attention to planting, protection of the trunk, which is usually wrapped in hessian for a few months, an individual irrigation system for the tree and underground guying or above-ground staking to support the tree until it becomes established. Post-planting weed control is also necessary (Wilson *et al.*, 2004). These authors consider some species within the genera *Acer, Malus, Platanus, Sorbus* and *Tilia* to be the most transplantable.

Ornamental trees

Where space is limited or where more decorative trees are required, trees from the families *Fabaceae*, e.g. *Laburnum, Gleditsia triacanthos* 'Sunburst'; *Rosaceae*, e.g. *Pyrus salicifolia* 'Pendula', *Malus* × *purpurea*; *Aceraceae*, e.g. *Acer davidii* and *A. griseum*; and *Betulaceae*, e.g. *Betula utilis* and *B. ermanii*, are appropriate.

Native or naturalistic-style planting

On difficult sites, such as embankments of motorways, derelict sites or reclaimed land, where nutrient levels are low and where access for staff and machinery is difficult, the use of whips and transplants is ideal. Such material is usually bare-rooted and care must be taken that roots do not dry out between lifting in the nursery and planting on site (Mc Evoy and McKay, 1997). Trees are notch-planted by digging a T or a slit in the soil, prising the slit apart and setting the whip or transplant into the slit and then closing it over with the heel of a boot.

A list of native trees and shrubs is given in Appendix 2, though it is advisable to check that these trees are native in the locality of any proposed planting scheme.

These techniques, along with seeding and natural regeneration, are used in the creation of urban woodland.

Staking of trees

Apart from whips and transplants, trees are staked on planting. The purpose is to hold the tree upright until the roots become established, gain anchorage in the soil and become wind-firm. Depending on the size of tree, budgets and access by the public to the site, the type of staking will vary (Table 5.4). Where trees are more than 2 m tall and above-ground staking is used, stakes should not extend beyond a third of the height of a tree (Patch, 1987) (Fig. 5.2). Stakes should be removed at the onset of the second growing season after planting. If a stake is left in place for a number of years, the tree becomes 'dependent' on the stake and will become lopsided if the stake is removed.

Management of trees

Grass and weeds are often described as 'hungry feeders', their roots competing with the roots of establishing trees for moisture and nutrients. In

Table 5.4. Types of tree staking.

Type of tree	Type of staking
Parkland	Below-ground guying with proprietary anchoring systems
Semi-mature tree	Above-ground guying with proprietary anchoring system with guys attached to subterranean stakes
	Propping of trees with a number of stakes arranged around the trunk of the tree just below the crown
Street trees	Below-ground guying with proprietary anchoring systems
	One or two short stakes attached to the tree with flexible ties
Amenity tree in shrubbery or ground-cover scheme	One or two short stakes attached to the tree with flexible ties
	Two short upright stakes linked by a T bar (Fig. 5.2)

Fig. 5.2. Two short stakes with the tree trunk attached to the cross-member by a rubber tie.

the early years of establishment, the ground at the base of the tree should be kept weed-free. Bradshaw *et al.* (1995) recommend weed control of 1 m in diameter around transplants and 1.5 m around standard trees. Inappropriate control of lawnmowers and Strimmers™ can result in damage to the bark at the base of the tree trunk.

Ties and stakes, when used, should be checked regularly. Loosen stakes and ensure that the stake is not damaging the bark (Fig. 5.3). Failure to do so renders trees more susceptible to disease and weakens the trunk and the tree will not develop satisfactorily (Brown, 1987).

Shrubs: Selection, Use and Management

Shrubs are described as woody plants with many stems and without a distinct trunk. They vary in size from prostrate low-growing shrubs to tall arboreal specimens some 10 m tall.

Depending on form, habit and growth rate, shrubs are used to create ground-cover schemes, to form hedges and hedgerows, to clothe walls and pergolas and to create large formal and informal shrubberies.

Ground-cover shrubs: selection, use and management

Ground-cover shrubs are defined as species or varieties of perennial woody or non-woody plants not exceeding 75 cm in height with a naturally prostrate, spreading or low-growing habit and moderate to rapid rates of growth to provide effective dense ground cover. Uses of ground-cover shrubs include weed suppression, soil stabilization, alternative or substitute for grass where grass would not grow or where it could not be maintained. Ground-cover

Fig. 5.3. A tree tie left in place for a long time, causes lasting damage to the tree trunk.

schemes have some disadvantages. Litter collects in schemes, especially ones with thorny plants, such as ground-cover roses. From a visual point of view, they can look dull and boring. They can be damaged due to excessive trampling and by people taking short cuts.

From a planting design point of view, such a scheme links and/or grades a planting scheme from tall shrubs down to ground level. It provides a scheme with contrasts of plant form, foliage colour and texture, flower colour and occasionally fruit (Fig. 5.4). Another form of ground cover, creating a carpet of flat vegetation is seen in Fig. 4.2.

The following categories of plants are used in ground-cover schemes: primarily evergreen shrubs, both broadleaved and coniferous, deciduous shrubs, herbaceous perennials and, very occasionally, rapid-growing annuals for instant effect are also used, though they are not treated here. The properties of effective ground-cover plants are ease of establishment, rapid

Fig. 5.4. Ground cover of mixed plant form and leaf textures.

growth after planting, resistance, reliability, low maintenance requirement and good all-year-round visual qualities. Finally, they will regenerate rapidly after pruning.

Selection of species and varieties

The following plant forms and habits are used as ground cover:

Thicket – mass of low-growing stems	*Lonicera pileata*
Carpet – dense mass of stems from ground level, often suckering	*Stephanandra incisa*
Sprawling shrubs tend to grow one into another	*Rubus tricolor*
Arching shrubs send up arching stems; they can look quite elegant but may not be very dense at the base	*Cotoneaster salicifolia* 'Repens'
Hummock – plants tend to stay as individuals	e.g. *Euonymus japonicus* 'Microphyllus'

A list of ground-cover plants is given in Appendix 3.

Planting centres and setting out

Spacing will depend on how soon a 'mature' effect is required; 3 to 5 years is a general requirement in most landscape schemes. Planting into weed-free soil is an essential for rapid establishment. So as to avoid a formal look, shrubs are generally planted in units of three, seven or nine plants, or multiples thereof. Mulch in the form of bark or green waste provides an instant unifier beneath newly planted shrubs, retains moisture and reduces weed growth.

For further reading on ground-cover schemes, see 'Shrubs and ground-cover' (Jakobsen, 1990) and 'Groundcover' (Thoday, 2004).

Hedges: Selection, Use and Management

Functions of hedges

Hedges direct traffic, act as a barrier to animals, provide a wildlife corridor, provide privacy for people, block unsightly objects and serve as windbreaks. On motorways low hedges protect against dazzle of oncoming traffic. From a design point of view, they define and create spaces. They act as a foil or backdrop for other plants and are attractive features in their own right. Evergreen, deciduous and flowering species are used to create hedges. Genera from three families in particular, *Caprifoliaceae*, *Oleaceae* and *Rosaceae*, provide most of the commonly grown hedging plants. The selection of particular species will depend on whether the hedge is formal or informal, the eventual size, large-growing (e.g. *Cotoneaster lacteus*) versus low-growing (e.g. *Buxus sempervirens*), location, whether it will withstand wind or frost damage and finally cost and availability. A list of hedging plants is given in Appendix 4.

Hedges: establishment and planting

1. Dig a trench 1–1.25 m wide; depending on the scale, use a spade, Bobcat or JCB.
2. Peg out a straight line and mark planting positions. Depending on the species, planting distance between plants varies between 30 and 60 cm. Plants can also be laid out in staggered or double rows.
3. Smaller material, usually bare-rooted, will establish more readily, but larger material, usually pot-grown or containerized, will give an instant effect. On a small scale, one plant per station is planted but, on a larger scale, such as motorway hedging or hedgerows, three plants are planted per station.

Some nurseries supply large specimens of prepared hedges such as *Taxus baccata* (yew) and *Fagus sylvatica* (beech).
4. Once planted tread bare-rooted material firmly and, with pot-grown material, firm well. Stake individual plants, especially when larger material has been planted. Prune straggly growth on planting.

In some situations a fence of chicken wire or other fencing material, with wooden or metal posts at intervals, is advisable to assist establishment and to prevent people from walking through the hedge.

In the first summer after planting prune shoots by a third and side shoots more severely. Gradually prune the hedge into a slightly 'A' shape, so that light will fall on the sides of the hedges. If a hedge is broader on top than at ground level, light will not reach the base of the hedge and it becomes thin and 'gappy'. Formal hedges are trimmed two to four times per year, informal once or twice per year.

Management of overgrown hedges

Prune in spring so that they will grow over the summer and will look least attractive for as short a time as possible. If necessary, mark out a line with white emulsion paint and cut with an electric hedge trimmer, or prune out with a chain saw and then, once it rejuvenates, prune with hedge trimmers. Prune one side one year and then the other side of the hedge in the succeeding year. The following can be pruned very hard, i.e. to bare wood: *Ligustrum ovalifolium, Buxus sempervirens, Lonicera nitida, Taxus baccata, Griselinia littoralis, Prunus laurocerasus* and *Laurus nobilis*. For further reading on hedges, see 'Hedges and their management' (Wright *et al.*, 2004).

Climbers: Selection, Use and Management

Climbers have a number of functional uses, including clothing a wall with vegetation, covering tree stumps or unsightly objects, and sprawling over rocks and pavements, where they can act as ground cover. Those grown on pergolas and trellises provide shade and shelter. Many climbing plants are decorative plants in their own right, providing attractive foliage, e.g. *Hydrangea anomala* subsp. *petiolaris*, flowers, e.g. *Wisteria* (*Fabaceae*), fruit, e.g. *Lonicera* (*Caprifoliaceae*), or autumn colour, e.g. *Parthenocissus quinquefolia*. Climbers have some disadvantages: leaves and roots block drains and pipes and some species can become rampant.

Based on their mode of growth and any support required, climbers are divided into three categories:

1. Self-clinging to walls, e.g. *Hedera*, which has aerial roots, and *Parthenocissus*, which has sucker pads.
2. Those climbers with twining stems, e.g. *Lonicera*, curling tendrils, e.g. *Vitis*, or curling petioles, e.g. *Clematis*, require the support of a trellis, pergola or other plants to support them as they grow.
3. Climbers known as scramblers, e.g. *Rosa filipes* 'Kiftsgate', which grow through trees.

Climbers often have to contend with poor growing conditions: a rain shadow at the base of a wall, bricks and mortar in the soil, inadequate depth of soil. When planting climbers, incorporate good-quality soil to a depth of 50 cm and plant some 15 to 30 cm from a wall.

Various types of support are provided for climbers. As well as providing support for climbers, a pergola or arbour is ornamental in its own right. Various types of trellis, including wooden, plastic, nylon and steel mesh, are available. Vertical or horizontal wires attached to a wall with a variety of wall nails are also available.

Of the families described in Chapter 4, only one, *Vitaceae*, provides climbing plants for temperate climates. Genera that include climbing plants are *Jasminum* (*Oleaceae*), *Lonicera* (*Caprifoliaceae*), *Hydrangea* (*Saxifragaceae*), *Solanum* (*Solanaceae*) and *Rosa* (*Rosaceae*).

For further information on climbers, see *The Collingridge Handbook of Climbing and Screening Plants* (Prockter, 1983) and 'Climbing plants' (La Dell, 2004).

Shrubs and Shrubberies

Many present-day landscape schemes in shopping centres, industrial parks and public open spaces consist of large drifts of shrubs (Fig. 5.1). Such schemes add structure and identity to an area and provide visual beauty and seasonal interest for passers-by.

Families from which come most of the shrubs cultivated in landscape schemes are listed in Table 5.5. Existing shrubberies, particularly in older public parks and inner-city gardens, where shrubs have survived on benign neglect for many years, are places to seek out genera for use in difficult situations. A list of such shrubs is given in Appendix 5.

In some situations a number of fast-growing, but short-lived shrubs are a useful 'nurse crop', as they provide visual interest, soil stabilization and weed smother and so on while other slower-growing shrubs become established. Most of these short-lived shrubs do not respond well to heavy pruning (Appendix 6). Another approach to the development of shrubberies, particularly where soil conditions are good and ornamental-style planting is appropriate, is to select shrubs with particular common characteristics, such as scent (Appendix 7), or those of particular interest at a certain time of the year, such as autumn or winter (Appendix 8 and Appendix 9).

With the predictions that changes in climate will result in higher temperatures and lower rainfall in summer and more extreme winter conditions of wind and floods, there is also an opportunity to grow more tender plants (Bisgrove and Hadley, 2002). Shrubs from the families *Asteraceae, Lamiaceae, Malvaceae, Myrtaceae* and *Solanaceae* are worth considering for dry, sun-baked areas with free-draining soil (Table 5.6). Where salt-laden wind predominates, trees and shrubs listed in Appendix 10 provide a first line of defence.

Table 5.5. Families providing shrubs for cultivation in landscape schemes.

Family	Common name	Tree	Shrubs	Climbers	Identification	Some native species	Common functions	Poor soil conditions	Deciduous/ evergreen	pH soil
Aquifoliaceae	Holly	X	X		Glossy, green, thorny foliage, red berries	X	Hedging, shrubbery	X	E	N
Berberidaceae	Berberis		X		Thorns on shoots, red/black berries	X	Hedging, shrubbery	X (some)	E/D	N
Buxaceae	Box		X		Small, elliptic leaves, with acrid smell	X	Hedging	X	E	N
Caprifoliaceae	Guelder rose		X	X	Tubular flowers, opposite leaves, juicy berries	X	Shrubbery	X (some)	D/E	N
Celastraceae	Spindle		X		Elliptic leaves, fruit three-cornered, pink, with orange seed within	X	Hedging, ground cover	X (some)	E/D	N
Cornaceae	Dogwood	X	X		Significant flowers, noticeable fruit/ berries	X	Shrubbery, specimen shrubs		E/D	N
Ericaceae	Heather		X		Often pitcher-shaped flower	X	Shrubbery, ground cover		E/D	<7
Fabaceae	Laburnum	X	X	X	Zygomorphic flower, often trifoliate leaf	X	Shrubbery, ground cover, especially in poor soil	X	D/E	N
Hamamelidaceae	Witch hazel		X		Large leaves with conspicuous veins. Medium to large shrub		Shrubbery, winter-flowering, autumn colour		D	N
Oleaceae	Olive	X	X	X	Tubular flower, entire or pinnate leaves	X	Shrubberies, scented plants, hedges	X (some)	D/E	N

Table 5.5. *Continued.*

Family	Common name	Tree	Shrubs	Climbers	Identification	Some native species	Common functions	Poor soil conditions	Deciduous/ evergreen	pH soil
Rhamnaceae	Ceanothus		X			X	Ground cover, shrubbery		E/D	N
Rosaceae	Rose	X	X	X	Alternate leaves, flowers/fruit	X	Ground cover, shrubbery, hedging	X (some)	D/E	N
Rutaceae	Mexican mock orange		X				Shrubbery		E	N
Saxifragaceae	Hydrangea, escallonia, currant		X				Hedging, shrubbery, ground cover		E/D	N

N, neutral soil, pH = 7.0.

Table 5.6. Families of tender shrubs suitable for sheltered sites and maritime areas.

Family	Common name	Tree	Shrubs	Climbers	Native	Maritime areas	Dry soil conditions	Identification	Grey foliage	Deciduous/ evergreen	pH soil
Asteraceae	Daisy		X		X	X	X (some)	Daisy-like flower	X (some)	E	N
Lamiaceae	Dead nettle		X		X	X	X	Square stems, opposite leaves	X (some)	E	N
Myrtaceae	Myrtle	X	X				X (some)	Flowers with a mass of stamens		E	< 7
Cistaceae	Rock rose		X			X	X	Large, single, open flowers, small to medium-sized shrubs	X (some)	E	N
Malvaceae	Mallow		X				X	Flowers funnel-shaped in shades of pink or mauve		E	N
Solanaceae	Potato		X	X				Potato flower or tubular flower		E	N

N, neutral soil, pH = 7.0.

Pruning of Shrubs

As a rule of thumb, most deciduous trees and shrubs can be pruned in the late autumn or early winter. Most evergreen shrubs are best pruned in early spring. Some shrubs flower on the current year's growth and are pruned after they have flowered, e.g. *Forsythia*. Others flower on older wood, e.g. *Chaenomeles*, and a framework of stems is retained from year to year. Roses (hybrid tea and floribunda) are pruned on an annual basis, general amenity shrubs on a less frequent basis.

Reasons for pruning include plant rejuvenation by removing any dead or diseased branches and encouraging young juvenile growth to renew the vigour of the shrub, which in turn leads to increased flower and fruit. Pruning also enhances the shape, form or habit of the shrub, known as formative pruning in trees, and keeps it within the scale of the overall scheme.

Before pruning any shrub, identify it:

When does it flower or fruit?
What function is it serving in a landscape scheme?
Will it withstand light, moderate or severe pruning?
What is the consequence of pruning on surrounding trees and shrubs?

If there are several old woody stems prune a few back to within centimetres of ground level, thereby encouraging new growth from the base of the plant. Where overgrown shrubs are concerned it may take a year or more to achieve the desired effect and there may be loss of flower or fruit for a season, but it will be worth it in the long run.

Further Investigation

Examination of growth rates of shrubs:

1. Select a planting scheme, for instance, a shrubbery or ground-cover scheme. If known, note the original planting date.
2. On graph paper or a grid with a scale of 1.50, show in plan the original planting positions of seven to ten shrubs in one section of the scheme.
3. Show how these plants have spread. Their footprint will vary not only between different kinds of shrubs but also among those of the same species.
4. Having shown the plants in plan, show the same selection of plants in elevation.
5. On the grid, code each plant with a letter or number.
6. On a separate sheet, give the name, spread and height of each plant and describe the habit, form and growth rate.
7. Finally, comment on whether you consider the original plant spacing was appropriate, too dense or too sparse.

References

Bassuk, N. and Whitlow, T. (1988) Environmental stress in street trees. *Arboricultural Journal* 12, 195–201.

Bird, R. (1994) *Lakeland Gardens*. Ward Lock, London.

Bisgrove, R. and Hadley, P. (2002) *Gardening in the Global Greenhouse: The Impacts of Climate Change on Gardens in the UK*. Technical Report, UKCIP, Oxford, UK.

Bradshaw, A., Hunt, B. and Walmsley, T. (1995) *Trees in the Urban Landscape: Principles and Practice*. E. and F.N. Spon, London.

Brown, I.R. (1987) Suffering at the stake. In: Patch, D. (ed.) *Advances in Practical Arboriculture*. HMSO, London, pp. 85–90.

Crowe, S. (1994) *Garden Design*, 3rd edn. Garden Art Press, Woodbridge, UK.

Dutton, G. (1997) *Some Branch against the Sky. The Practice and Principles of Marginal Gardening*. David and Charles, Newton Abbot, UK.

Edwards, T. and Gale, T. (2004) Trees in paving. In: Hitchmough, J. and Fieldhouse, K. (eds) *Plant User Handbook: A Guide to Effective Specifying*. Blackwell Science, Oxford, UK, pp. 143–151.

Goulding, B. (1982) Twelve elegant fallacies for woodland gardens. *Moorea* 1, 21–36.

Hill, D. (1968) A painter's garden: St Colomb's in Donegal. *Journal of the Royal Horticultural Society* 93, 219–222.

HTA (2002) *National Plant Specification*. Horticultural Trades Association, Reading, UK.

Jakobsen, P. (1990) Shrubs and groundcover. In: Clouston, B. (ed.) *Landscape Design with Plants*, 2nd edn. Butterworth Architecture, Oxford, UK, pp. 40–75.

James, N.D.G. (1990) *The Arboriculturalist's Companion: A guide to the Care of Trees*, 2nd edn. Basil Blackwell, Oxford, UK.

La Dell, T. (2004) Climbing plants. In: Hitchmough, J. and Fieldhouse, K. (eds) *Plant User Handbook: A Guide to Effective Specifying*. Blackwell Science, Oxford, UK, pp. 211–220.

McEvoy, C. and McKay, H. (1997) *Sensitivity of Broadleaved Trees to Desiccation and Rough Handling Between Lifting and Transplanting*. Arboriculture Research and Information Note, Arboricultural Advisory and Information Service, Farnham, UK.

McKay, H. (1997) Try before you buy. *Horticulture Week* 23 January, 22–23.

McMahon, B. (1992) *The Master*. Poolbeg, Swords, Dublin.

Patch, D. (1987) Trouble at the stake. In: Patch, D. (ed.) *Advances in Practical Arboriculture*. HMSO, London, pp. 77–84.

Pauliet, S., Jones, N., Garcia-Martin, G., Garcia-Valdecantos, J.L., Rivière, L.M., Vidal-Beaudet, L., Bodson, M. and Randrup, T. (2002) Tree establishment practice in towns and cities – results from a European survey. *Urban Forestry and Urban Greening* 1, 83–96.

Prockter, N. (1983) *The Collingridge Handbook of Climbing and Screening Plants*. Collingridge, Feltham, UK.

Robinson, N. (2004) *Plant Design Handbook*, 2nd edn. Ashgate, Aldershot, UK.

Thoday, P. (2004) Groundcover. In: Hitchmough, J. and Fieldhouse, K. (eds) *Plant User Handbook: A Guide to Effective Specifying*. Blackwell Science, Oxford, UK, pp.175–183.

Trowbridge, P.J. and Bassuk, N.L. (2004) *Trees in the Urban Landscape: Site Assessment, Design, and Installation*. Wiley, Hoboken, New Jersey.

Waterfield, M. (1907) *Flower Grouping in English, Scotch and Irish Gardens*. J.M. Dent, London.

Wilson, J., Swann, C. and Thoday, P. (2004) Semi-mature trees. In: Hitchmough, J. and Fieldhouse, K. (eds) *Plant User Handbook: A Guide to Effective Specifying*, Blackwell Science, Oxford, UK, pp. 128–142.

Wright, T., Henry, T. and Bultitude, J. (2004) Hedges and their management. In: Hitchmough, J. and Fieldhouse, K. (eds) *Plant User Handbook: A Guide to Effective Specifying*. Blackwell Science, Oxford, UK, pp. 184–193.

Glossary

anther upper portion of the stamen, the pollen (male organ) in a flower

aril a fleshy appendage partly covering a seed, e.g. *Taxus baccata*

auricle refers to an ear-shaped lobe at the base of a leaf, near the petiole, e.g. *Quercus robur*

awl-shaped leaves: leaves that taper to a sharp point

axil angle formed by a leaf and a stem or where the veins of a leaf meet

axillary refers to the area between the main stem and a side shoot or in shrubs or trees it refers to the side growth as opposed to the top or terminal growth

berry a type of fruit with pulp and several seeds

bract a modified leaf occurring at the base of a flower or shoot

catkin dense spike of tiny flowers or fruits

container-grown plant which has been growing in a container for a sufficient time for the roots to have grown satisfactorily but not become pot-bound

coppiced stems are cut to within a few centimetres of ground level

corolla the petals of a flower, in various shapes, petals either free, each one separate, as in a rose, or united to form a tube (tubular) (*Lonicera*) or bell shape (campanulate) or funnel-shaped flowers

corymb a flat-topped shape of flower, outer flowers open first

cuneate a narrowing, tapering shape at the base of a leaf.

cupule form of seed capsule in *Fagus*

cyme a flat-topped shape of flower, where inner flowers open first

deciduous loses leaves in winter

drupe a fleshy fruit enclosing one or more seeds, e.g. *Prunus* (plum or sloe)

elliptic/ellipsoid: ellipse-shaped, i.e. widest at the middle and narrowing at either end of the leaf

entire leaf blade without lobes or any divisions or thorns

epicormic growth: shoots developing from ground level or from the trunk of a tree.

evergreen holds leaves in winter

© M. Forrest 2006. *Landscape Trees and Shrubs: Selection, Use and Management* (M. Forrest)

felted hairy, dense covering on either the upper or the lower surface of a leaf or both

fluted trunk: with rounded ridges running vertically

glabrous without hairs

globose globular, globe-shaped

inflorescence overall flower, composed of corolla (petals), sepals, stamens and stigma, style and ovary

lanceolate lance-shaped leaves

lobed leaves divided into segments

monotypic a family or genus with one genus in the family or one species in a genus

ovoid egg-shaped

palmately lobed lobed or divided in the shape of a hand, usually five or seven segments

panicle a branched raceme, usually conical in outline

pendulous hanging or drooping

petiole stalk between stem and leaf blade

phytophagous foliage-eating insects

pinnate leaf: leaf with a number of leaflets (pinnae)

raceme type of flower spike where each individual flower has a short stalk

radially symmetric flower where a flower can be divided on many axes

root-balled root-ball is lifted, wrapped in material such as hessian and remains intact until replanted

sepals part of flower below the corolla

serrated margins of leaf: leaf looks as if it was trimmed with pinking shears

spine a thorn or prickle, seen on the margins of leaves or on stems or shoots

sport an atypical shoot growing on a plant, which is often propagated and put into the trade as a new cultivar

stamen composed of anther and filament, male organ of a flower

stigma part of the female organ where the pollen lands and then moves down the style to the ovary

stipules leafy growth at the base of a leaf

stomata pores occuring on the undersurface of the leaf; white bands of stomata are conspicuous on *Picea* and *Abies* in particular

strobilus, strobili: male 'flowers' on conifers

tendril adapted leaf allowing a plant to climb and twine around other shrubs

terminal at the extremity of the plant refers to the location of an inflorescence

undulate wavy

whorl flowers, leaves and cones arranged in a ring around a stem or shoot

zygomorphic flower that can only be divided in two in one axis

Appendices

Appendix 1   Parkland Trees

Aesculus × carnea
Aesculus hippocastanum   Horse chestnut
Aesculus indica   Indian horse chestnut
Castanea sativa   Sweet chestnut
Fagus sylvatica   Beech
F. sylvatica Atropurpurea Group   Purple or copper beech
F. sylvatica 'Dawyck'
F. sylvatica var. *heterophylla*   Fern-leaved beech
F. sylvatica 'Pendula'   Weeping beech
F. sylvatica 'Purpurea'
F. sylvatica 'Zlatia'
Fraxinus excelsior   Ash
F. excelsior 'Pendula'   Weeping ash
F. ornus
Juglans regia   Common walnut
Platanus × hispanica   London plane
Platanus orientalis   Oriental plane
Populus canescens   Grey poplar
P. nigra 'Italica'   Lombardy poplar
Pterocarya fraxinifolia   Wing nut
Quercus cerris   Turkey oak
Quercus ilex   Evergreen oak
Quercus petraea   Sessile oak
Quercus robur   English oak
Salix alba   Willow
Tilia × euchlora
Tilia × europaea   Lime
Ulmus glabra   Elm

© M. Forrest 2006. *Landscape Trees and Shrubs: Selection, Use and Management* (M. Forrest)

Appendix 2   Native Trees and Shrubs in Britain and Ireland*

Acer campestre	Field maple (Britain)
Alnus glutinosa	Alder
Betula pendula	Birch
Betula pubescens	Birch
Cornus alba	Dogwood
Corylus avellana	Hazel
Crataegus laevigata	Hawthorn
Crataegus monogyna	Hawthorn
Euonymus europaeus	Spindle
Fraxinus excelsior	Ash
Ilex aquifolium	Holly
Populus tremula	Poplar
Prunus spinosa	Blackthorn
Rhamnus frangula	Alder, buckthorn
Rosa canina	Dog rose
Rosa spinosissima	Burnet rose
Rubus fruticosus	Bramble
Salix	Willow
Sambucus nigra	Elder
Sorbus aria	Whitebeam
Sorbus aucuparia	Rowan, mountain ash
Viburnum lantana	Wayfaring tree (Britain)
Viburnum opulus	Guelder rose
Ulex europaeus	Gorse, whin, furze
Ulmus glabra	Wych elm
Ulmus procera	Elm (Britain)

Appendix 3   Selection of Ground-cover Plants

Broadleaved shrubs

Berberis candidula
Berberis thunbergii f. *atropurpurea*
Brachyglottis monroi
Brachyglottis 'Sunshine'
Ceanothus rigidus 'Snowball'
Ceanothus thrysiflorus var. *repens*
Chaenomeles japonica
Cotoneaster dammeri
Cotoneaster horizontalis
Cotoneaster salicifolia 'Repens'

* Few of the species listed occur throughout Britain and Ireland and a local flora should be consulted before introducing a non-local species to an area.

Erica carnea 'Springwood Spring'
E. carnea 'Springwood White'
Euonymus fortunei
E. fortunei 'Radicans'
Genista lydia
Hedera helix
Lavandula officinalis
Lonicera pileata
Pachysandra terminalis
Potentilla fruticosa
Potentilla 'Tangerine'
Rosa 'Nozomi'
Rosa paulii
Rosa rugosa cultivars
Rosa 'Rutland'
Rosmarinus officinalis Prostratus Group
Rubus rolfei
Rubus tricolor
Sarcococca ruscifolia
Skimmia japonica
Symphoricarpos × *chenaultii* 'Hancock'

Conifers

Juniperus communis
Picea abies 'Nidiformis'
Pinus mugo 'Mops'
Taxus baccata 'Semperaurea'

Appendix 4   Hedging Plants

Deciduous species

Berberis thunbergii 'Atropurpurea'
Carpinus betulus   Hornbeam
Crataegus monogyna   Hawthorn
Fagus sylvatica   Beech
Prunus 'Cistena'

Evergreen species

Buxus sempervirens   Box
Euonymus japonicus
Grisilinia littoralis

Ilex aquifolium   Holly
Laurus nobilis   Bay laurel
Ligustrum ovalifolium   Privet
L. ovalifolium 'Aureum'
Lonicera nitida
Lonicera nitida 'Baggesen's Gold'
Lonicera pileata
Pittosporum tenuifolium
Prunus laurocerasus   Cherry Laurel
Taxus baccata   Yew

Flowering species

Cotoneaster lacteus
Cotoneaster simonsii
Escallonia 'Apple Blossom'
Escallonia macrantha
Forsythia × intermedia
Fuchsia magellanica
Fuchsia 'Mrs Popple'
Lavandula officinalis   Lavender
Pyracantha rogersiana
Rosa spp.

Appendix 5   Tough, Reliable Shrubs

They survive on minimum maintenance and will withstand pruning. They are
common in suburban gardens and public parks and open spaces in inner-city
Dublin (for which one could substitute other cities in Britain and Ireland and
Western Europe).
Aucuba japonica 'Variegata'
Berberis darwinii
Buxus sempervirens
Chaenomeles japonica
Cornus alba
Cornus sericea
Cotoneaster horizontalis
Euonymus japonicus and cultivars
Fatsia japonica
Forsythia
Hedera helix
Hydrangea macrophylla
Ilex aquifolium and cultivars
Jasminum nudiflorum
Ligustrum ovalifolium

Lonicera nitida
Osmanthus heterophyllus
Prunus laurocerasus
Pyracantha spp. and cultivars
Rhododendron (those known as 'Hardy Hybrids')
Ribes sanguineum
Rubus tricolor
Ruscus aculeatus
Sambucus nigra
Sambucus racemosa
Skimmia japonica
Spiraea 'Arguta'
Taxus baccata
Viburnum tinus

Appendix 6   Short-lived Shrubs

These are fast-growing and valuable for a few years but do not respond well to heavy pruning.
Ceanothus spp.
Cytisus
Genista
Hebe (small-leaved species and cultivars)
Lavandula
Lupinus arboreus
Ozothamnus ledifolius

Appendix 7 Shrubs with Scented Flowers and Foliage

Escallonia macrantha
Eucalyptus spp.
Hamamelis mollis
Jasminum officinale
Lavandula officinalis
Lonicera periclymenum
Lonicera standishii
Roses (some are highly scented)
Rosmarinus officinalis
Sarcococca spp.
Syringa vulgaris
Ulex europaeus

Appendix 8   Ornamental Autumn Interest

Shrubs and trees for autumn colour

Acer japonicum
Acer palmatum
Cercidiphyllum japonicum
Cornus florida
Euonymus alatus
Euonymus europaeus
Fothergilla monticola
Hamamelis mollis
Parrotia persica
Parthenocissus tricuspidata
Prunus serrulata
Sorbus thuringiaca
Viburnum plicatum

Shrubs and trees for autumn berries and fruits

Aesculus hippocastanum
Castanea sativa
Cotoneaster horizontalis
Crataegus monogyna
Malus × *zumi* 'Golden Hornet'
Pyracantha rogersiana
Rosa rugosa
Sorbus hupehensis
Sorbus × *intermedia*
Sorbus 'Joseph Rock'

Appendix 9   Shrubs and Trees for Winter Interest

Bark effect

Acer capillipes
Acer davidii
Acer griseum
Acer palmatum 'Sango-kaku'
Acer pensylvanicum
Arbutus andrachne
Betula albosinensis var. *septentrionalis*
Betula ermannii
Cornus alba
Prunus serrula

Flowering shrubs and trees

Alnus glutinosa
Alnus incana ' Rubra'
Correa 'Mannii'
Garrya elliptica
Hamamelis mollis
Jasminum nudiflorum
Lonicera standishii
Mahonia 'Charity'
Mahonia lomariifolia
Parrotia persica
Prunus subhirrtella 'Autumnalis'
Ribes laurifolium
Sarcococca confusa
Sarcococca ruscifolia
Viburnum 'Bodnantense'
Viburnum farreri
Viburnum farreri 'Candidissimum'
Viburnum tinus

Winter berries

Cotoneaster horizontalis
Cotoneaster 'Hybridus Pendulus'
Cotoneaster lacteus
Ilex × altaclerensis 'Golden King'
Ilex aquifolium 'Silver Queen'
Pyracantha 'Orange Glow'
Pyracantha rogersiana
Skimmia japonica
Taxus baccata

Appendix 10 Shrubs and Trees in Maritime Areas

Acer pseudoplatanus
Cordyline australis
× *Cupressocyparis leylandii*
Cupressus macrocarpa
Escallonia macrantha and cultivars
Eucalyptus spp.
Fuchsia magellanica
Griselinia littoralis
Hippophae rhamnoides
Olearia macrodonta

Olearia traversii
Phormium tenax
Pinus radiata
Pittosporum tenuifolium
Quercus ilex
Rhododendron ponticum (position with care as it will become naturalized in
    some locations)
Rosa rugosa

Bibliography

Anon. (1999) Carbon storage in Edinburgh. *landlines* 102, August 1999.

Anon. (2003) *The Hillier Manual of Trees and Shrubs*. David and Charles, Newton Abbot, UK.

Argent, G., Bond, J., Chamberlain, D., Cox, P. and Hardy, A. (1997) *The Rhododendron Handbook 1998*. Royal Horticultural Society, London.

Arnold-Foster, W. (1948) *Shrubs for the Milder Counties*, Country Life, London. [2000 edition published by Alison Hodge, Bosulval, Newmill, Penzance, Cornwall.]

Bassuk, N. and Whitlow, T. (1988) Environmental stress in street trees. *Arboricultural Journal* 12, 195–201.

Bean, W.J. (1970–1988) *Trees and Shrubs Hardy in the British Isles*, 8th edn. John Murray, London.

Bird, R. (1994) *Lakeland Gardens*. Ward Lock, London.

Bisgrove, R. and Hadley, P. (2002) *Gardening in the Global Greenhouse: The Impacts of Climate Change on Gardens in the UK*. Technical Report. UKCIP, Oxford, UK.

Booth, N.K. (1983) *Basic Elements of Landscape Architectural Design*. Elsevier, New York.

Bradshaw, A., Hunt, B. and Walmsley, T. (1995) *Trees in the Urban Landscape: Principles and Practice*. E. and F.N. Spon, London.

Brander, P.E. (1995) *Tilia* (lind) til alléer, aprk og anlæg – et alternative til elm. *Grøn viden* 88 (September), 1–6. [In Danish.]

Brickell, C., Baum, B.R., Hetterschneid, W.L.A., Leslie, A.C., McNeill, J., Trehane, P., Vrugtman, F. and Wiersema, J.H. (eds) (2004) *International Code for Nomenclature for Cultivated Plants*, 7th edn. Acta Horticulturae, 647, International Society for Horticultural Science, Leuven, Belgium.

Broadmeadow, M. and Freer-Smith, P. (1996) *Urban Woodland and the Benefits for Local Air Quality*. HMSO, London.

Brown, I.R. (1987) Suffering at the stake. In: Patch, D. (ed.) *Advances in Practical Arboriculture*. HMSO, London, pp. 85–90.

Cappiello, P. and Shadow, D. (2005) *Dogwoods: The Genus Cornus*. Timber Press, Portland, Oregon.

Chadbund, G. (1972) *Flowering Cherries*. Collins, London.

Coppin, N. and Stiles, R. (1990) The use of vegetation in slope stabilization. In: Clouston, B. (ed.) *Landscape Design with Plants*. Butterworth Architecture, Oxford, UK, pp. 212–234.

Crowe, S. (1994) *Garden Design*, 3rd edn. Garden Art Press, Woodbridge,UK.

Cullen, J. (1997) *The Identification of Flowering Plant Families*. Cambridge University Press, Cambridge, UK.

Cullen, J. (2001) *Handbook of European Garden Plants*. Cambridge University Press. Cambridge, UK.

Dutton, G. (1997) *Some Branch against the Sky: The Practice and Principles of Marginal Gardening*. David and Charles, Newton Abbot, UK.

Edwards, T. and Gale, T. (2004) Trees in paving. In: Hitchmough, J. and Fieldhouse, K. (eds) *Plant User Handbook: A Guide to Effective Specifying*. Blackwell Science, Oxford, UK, pp. 143–151.

Fiala, J. (1995) *Flowering Crabapples: The Genus* Malus. Timber Press, Portland, Oregon.

Fiala, J. (2002) *Lilacs: The Genus* Syringa. Timber Press, Portland, Oregon.

Forrest, M. (2004) The introduction of oak species into Britain and Ireland. *International Oaks* 15, 82–93.

Galle, F.C. (1997) *Hollies: The Genus* Ilex. Timber Press, Portland, Oregon.

Gardiner, J. (2000) *Magnolias: A Gardener's Guide*. Timber Press, Portland, Oregon.

Gasson, P.E. and Cutler, D.F. (1998) Can we live with trees in our towns and cities? *Arboricultural Journal* 22, 1–9.

Goulding, B. (1982) Twelve elegant fallacies for woodland gardens. *Moorea* 1, 21–36.

Grahn, P. and Stigsdotter, U.A. (2003) Landscape planning and stress. *Urban Forestry and Urban Greening* 2, 1–18.

Greuter, W., McNeill, J., Barrie, F.R., Burdet, H.-M., Demoulin, V., Filgueiras, T.S., Nicolson, D.H., Silva, P.C., Skog, J.E., Trehane, P., Turland, N.J. and Hawksworth, D.L. (2000) *International Code of Botanical Nomenclature (St Louis Code)*. Regnum Vegetabile, 138, Koeltz Scientific Books, Köningstein, Germany.

Halpenny, K. and Simms, W. (2005) The national collection of shrubby potentillas at Ardgillan Demesne, Balbriggan, Co. Dublin. *Moorea* 14, 17–22.

Hickey, M. and King, C. (1997) *Common Families of Flowering Plants*. Cambridge University Press, Cambridge, UK.

Hill, D. (1968) A painter's garden: St Colomb's in Donegal. *Journal of the Royal Horticultural Society* 93, 219–222.

Hitchmough, J. (1996) Where are the new plants to come from? Harnessing nature and science. In: Thoday, P. and Wilson, J. (eds) *Landscape Plants*. Cheltenham and Gloucester College of Higher Education, Cheltenham, UK, pp. 21–30.

HTA (2002) *National Plant Specification*. Horticultural Trades Association, Reading, UK.

Innes, J.L. (1990) Plants and air pollution. In: Clouston, B. (ed.) *Landscape Design with Plants*. Butterworth Architecture, Oxford, UK, pp. 199–211.

Jablonskii, E. (2004) European oak cultivars, collections and collectors. *International Oaks* 15, 103–118.

Jakobsen, P. (1990) Shrubs and groundcover. In: Clouston, B. (ed.) *Landscape Design with Plants*, 2nd edn. Butterworth Architecture, Oxford, UK, pp. 40–75.

James, N.D.G. (1990) *The Arboriculturalist's Companion: A Guide to the Care of Trees*, 2nd edn. Basil Blackwell, Oxford, UK.

La Dell, T. (2004) Climbing plants. In: Hitchmough, J. and Fieldhouse, K. (eds) *Plant User Handbook: A Guide to Effective Specifying*. Blackwell Science, Oxford, UK, pp. 211–220.

Land Use Consultants (1993) *Trees in Towns: A Survey of Trees in 66 Towns and Villages in England*. Research for Amenity Trees No.1, HMSO, London.

Lane, C. (2005) *Witch Hazels*. Timber Press, Portland, Oregon.

Lord, T. (ed.) (2005) *RHS Plant Finder 2005–2006*. Dorling Kindersley, London.

McEvoy, C. and McKay, H. (1997) *Sensitivity of Broadleaved Trees to Desiccation and Rough Handling Between Lifting and Transplanting*. Arboriculture Research and Information Note, Arboricultural Advisory and Information Service, Farnham, UK.

McKay, H. (1997) Try before you buy. *Horticulture Week* 23 January, 22–23.

McMahon, B. (1992) *The Master*. Poolbeg, Swords, Dublin.

Mitchell, A. (2001) *Collins Field Guide: Trees of Britain and Northern Europe*. Collins, London.

Newsholme, C. (2003) *Willows: The Genus Salix*. Timber Press, Portland, Oregon.

Nowak, D.J. (1993) Atmospheric carbon reduction by urban trees. *Journal of Environmental Management* 37, 207–217.

Nowak, D.J. and Dwyer, J.F. (2000) Understanding the benefits and costs of urban forest ecosystems. In: Kuser, J.E. (ed.) *Handbook of Urban and Community Forestry in the Northeast*. Kluwer Academic/Plenum Publishers, New York, pp. 11–25.

Patch, D. (1987) Trouble at the stake. In: Patch, D. (ed.) *Advances in Practical Arboriculture*. HMSO, London, pp. 77–84.

Patch, D. (1998) *Trees, Shelter and Energy Conservation*. Arboricultural Research Note 145/Arb/98, DOE, Arboricultural Advisory and Information Service, Farnham, UK.

Pauliet, S., Jones, N., Garcia-Martin, G., Garcia-Valdecantos, J.L., Rivière, L.M., Vidal-Beaudet, L., Bodson, M. and Randrup, T. (2002) Tree establishment practice in towns and cities – results from a European survey. *Urban Forestry and Urban Greening* 1, 83–96.

Phillips, R. and Rix, M. (2004) *Ultimate Guide to Roses: A Comprehensive Selection*. Macmillan, London.

Phipps, J. (2003) *Hawthorns and Medlars*. Timber Press, Portland, Oregon.

Prockter, N. (1983) *The Collingridge Handbook of Climbing and Screening Plants*. Collingridge, Feltham, UK.

Robinson, N. (2004) *Planting Design Handbook*, 2nd edn. Ashgate, Aldershot, UK.

Saebø, A., Borzan, Ž., Ducatillion, C., Hatzistathis, A., Lagerström, T., Supuka, J., Garcia-Valdecantos, J.L., Rego, F. and Van Slycken, J. (2005) The selection of plant materials for street trees, park trees and urban woodland. In: Konijnendijk, C., Nilsson, K., Randrup, T. and Schipperijn, J. (eds) *Urban Forests and Trees*. Springer, Berlin, pp. 257–280.

Savill, P.S. (1991) *The Silviculture of Trees Used in British Forestry*. CAB International, Wallingford, UK.

Scannell, M. and Synnott, D. (1987) *Census Catalogue of the Flora of Ireland*, 2nd edn. Stationery Office, Dublin.

Stearn, W.T. (1992) *Stearn's Dictionary of Plant Names for Gardeners*. Cassell, London.

Tello, M.-L., Tomalek, M., Siwecki, R., Gáper, J., Motta, E. and Mateo-Sagasta, E. (2005) Biotic urban growing conditions – threats, pests and diseases. In: Konijnendijk, C., Nilsson, K., Randrup, T. and Schipperijn, J. (eds) *Urban Forests and Trees*. Springer, Berlin, pp. 325–365.

Thoday, P. (1996) Landscape plants. In: Thoday, P. and Wilson, J. (eds) *Landscape Plants*. Cheltenham and Gloucester College of Higher Education, Cheltenham, UK, pp.1–9.

Thoday, P. (2004) Groundcover. In: Hitchmough, J. and Fieldhouse, K. (eds) *Plant User Handbook: A Guide to Effective Specifying*. Blackwell Science, Oxford, UK, pp.175–183.

Treseder, N. (1978) *Magnolias*. Faber & Faber, London.

Trowbridge, P.J. and Bassuk, N.L. (2004) *Trees in the Urban Landscape: Site Assessment, Design, and Installation*. Wiley, Hoboken, New Jersey.

Ulrich, R.S., Simons, R.F., Losito, B.D., Fiorito, E., Miles, M.A. and Zelson, M. (1991) Stress recovery during exposure to natural and urban environments. *Journal of Environmental Psychology* 11, 201–230.

Underhill, D. (1971) *Heaths and Heathers*. David and Charles, Newton Abbot, UK.

Upson, T. and Andrews, S. (2004) *The Genus Lavandula*. Royal Botanic Gardens, Kew, London.

Van Gelderen, C.J. and Van Gelderen, D.M. (1999) *Maples for Gardens*, Timber Press, Portland, Oregon.

Van Gelderen, D.M., de Jong, P.C. and Oterdoom, H.J. (1994) *Maples of the World*. Timber Press, Portland, Oregon.

Vertrees, J.D. and Gregory, P. (2001) *Japanese Maples*. Timber Press, Portland, Oregon.

Walter, K. (2001) Overview of the living collection at RBGE. In: Govier, R., Walter, K., Chamberlain, D., Gardner, M., Thomas, P., Alexander, C., Maxwell, H. and Watson, M. (eds) *Catalogue of Plants 2001*. Royal Botanic Garden Edinburgh, Edinburgh, pp. ix–xxiii.

Waterfield, M. (1907) *Flower Grouping in English, Scotch and Irish Gardens*. J.M. Dent, London.

Wilson, J., Swann, C. and Thoday, P. (2004) Semi-mature trees. In: Hitchmough, J. and Fieldhouse, K. (eds) *Plant User Handbook: A Guide to Effective Specifying*. Blackwell Science, Oxford, UK, pp. 128–142.

Wong, T.W., Good, J.E.G. and Denne, M.P. (1988) Tree root damage to pavements and kerbs in the city of Manchester. *Arboricultural Journal* 12, 17–34.

Wright, T., Henry, T. and Bultitude, J. (2004) Hedges and their management. In : Hitchmough, J. and Fieldhouse, K. (eds) *Plant User Handbook: A Guide to Effective Specifying*. Blackwell Science, Oxford, UK, pp. 184–193.

Yates, D. and McKennan, G. (1988) Solar architecture and light attenuation by trees: conflict or compromise? *Landscape Research* 13(1), 19–23.

Index of planting schemes and landscape trees and shrubs by country

Numbers in *italics* indicate illustrations

Index of pests and diseases

Plant Index

Page numbers in **bold** indicate the most important page references to a genus
Page numbers in *italics* indicate illustrations